Microsoft®

ACCESS 2003

Copyright - Editions ENI - May 2005
ISBN : 2-7460-2820-4
Original edition: 2-7460-2190-0

Editions ENI

BP 32125
44021 NANTES Cedex 01 - France

Phone: +33 (0)2 51 80 15 15
Fax: +33 (0)2 51 80 15 16

E-mail: info@eni-publishing.com
http: www.eni-publishing.com

Straight to the Point collection directed by Corinne HERVO

Foreword

The aim of this book is to let you find rapidly how to perform any task in the relational database management system **Access 2003**.
The final pages are given over to an **index** of the topics covered.

The typographic conventions used in this book are as follows:

Typefaces used for specific purposes:

bold   indicates the option to take in a menu or dialog box.

italic   is used for notes and comments.

Ctrl   represents a key from the keyboard; when two keys appear side by side, they should be pressed simultaneously.

Symbols indicating the content of a paragraph:

▷   an action to carry out (activating an option, clicking with the mouse...).

⇨   a general comment on the command in question.

⌀   a technique which involves the mouse.

A   a keyboard technique.

▨   a technique which uses options from the menus.

Table
of **Content**

QUERIES

TABLES AND CHARTS

MACROS

COMMUNICATION

INDEX

1 The Access environment

A - Starting/leaving Access 2003

Starting Access 2003

> Click the **start** button, drag to the **All Programs** option, then **Microsoft Office**, then click **Microsoft Office Access 2003**.

*The Access application window appears on the screen. You can see the **Getting Started** task pane at the right of the window.*

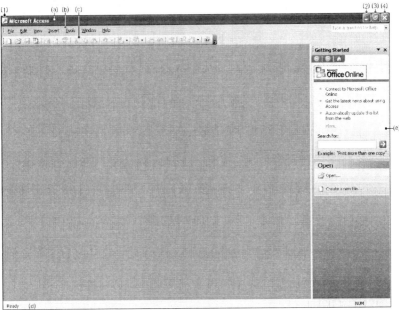

*In the **Getting Started** task pane, Access gives you the opportunity to open an existing database, create a blank database or create a database from an existing file or a template.*

(a) The **title bar**, with the **Control** menu icon (1) and the **Minimize** (2), **Restore** (3) (or **Maximize** ▣) and **Close** (4) buttons.

(b) The **menu bar**, which contains the names of all the menus within the Access application.

(c) The **Database toolbar**, whose tools are used to carry out certain commands quickly.

(d) The **status bar**, which displays information relating to the current task.

(e) The **task pane** contains options for carrying out various tasks, such as creating a new database, searching for files and so on. By default, the **Getting Started** task pane appears when you open the Microsoft Access application.

⇒ *A shortcut in the form of an icon may be installed on the Windows desktop; double-clicking this shortcut will start the application.*

Leaving Access 2003

▷ **File**   Click the button   Alt F4
   Exit   on the application window

▷ If you try to leave Access 2003 without saving any changes you have made to open objects, an error message appears. Click **Yes** to save your changes and leave Access, click **No** to leave Access without saving the changes, or click **Cancel** to not save but keep Access open.

B- Managing the task pane

▷ To display the task pane, use the **View - Task Pane** command or Ctrl F1.

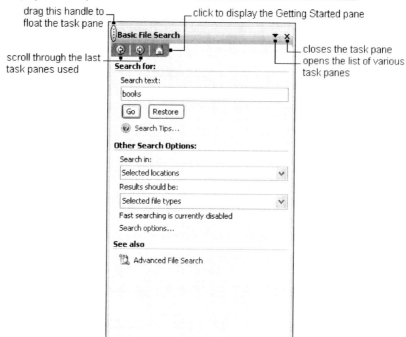

drag this handle to float the task pane

click to display the Getting Started pane

scroll through the last task panes used

closes the task pane
opens the list of various task panes

C- Undoing actions

▷ To undo your last action, use **Edit - Undo** or ↺ or Ctrl Z.

▷ To undo several previous actions, click the down arrow on the ↺▾ tool button, then click the earliest action you want to undo.

⇨ *If you have second thoughts, you can use ↻▾ to redo the actions you have just cancelled!*

⇨ *You can also undo several actions by clicking the ↺ tool button as many times as necessary.*

D-Finding help on Access features

If your Internet connection is online, Word searches on the Microsoft Office Online web site, which ensures that you have up-to-date information.

Searching with keywords

▷ Open the **Access Help** task pane by pressing `F1` on the keyboard.

▷ Enter the search keywords in the **Search for** text box and click the ⮕ button.

The titles of help topics that match your keywords appear in the ***Search Results*** *task pane.*

▷ Click the link for the required help topic to display the corresponding help text.

The ***Microsoft Office Access Help*** *window appears on the screen.*

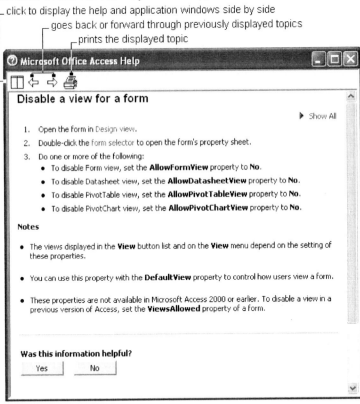

click to display the help and application windows side by side
goes back or forward through previously displayed topics
prints the displayed topic

Microsoft Office Access Help

Disable a view for a form

▶ Show All

1. Open the form in Design view.
2. Double-click the form selector to open the form's property sheet.
3. Do one or more of the following:
    - To disable Form view, set the **AllowFormView** property to **No**.
    - To disable Datasheet view, set the **AllowDatasheetView** property to **No**.
    - To disable PivotTable view, set the **AllowPivotTableView** property to **No**.
    - To disable PivotChart view, set the **AllowPivotChartView** property to **No**.

Notes

- The views displayed in the **View** button list and on the **View** menu depend on the setting of these properties.

- You can use this property with the **DefaultView** property to control how users view a form.

- These properties are not available in Microsoft Access 2000 or earlier. To disable a view in a previous version of Access, set the **ViewsAllowed** property of a form.

Was this information helpful?

Yes   No

▷ To make a new search, enter the required keyword(s) in the text box in the **Search** frame, at the bottom of the **Search Results** task pane, and click the ⮕ button to start searching.

▷ Once you have finished, click the ⊠ button to close the help window.

⇨ *You can also make a keyword search using the **Type a question for help*** `Type a question for help` *text box on the right hand end of the menu bar; click the box then enter a question or keyword.*

Searching in the Table of Contents

▷ Open the **Access Help** task pane with `F1` then click the **Table of Contents** link located in the **Assistance** frame.

▷ To expand a category of topics, click the corresponding "closed book" 📖. To display the required help topic, click its 📄 icon.

*The details of the chosen help text appear in the **Microsoft Office Access Help** window (cf. the previous subheading).*

▷ Once you have finished with the help text, click the ⊠ button to close the help window.

⇨ *You can also search for help with the Office Assistant **(Help - Show the Office Assistant)**, but first you need to install the Office Assistant component.*

⇨ *The links located in the **Office Online** frame of the **Access Help** task pane give you Internet access to Microsoft online services, where you can get technical support, download extras such as clip art or templates, or take online tutorials.*

1.2 Toolbars

A- Showing/hiding a toolbar

▷ **View - Toolbars**

▷ Click the name of the toolbar that you wish to show or hide (when a toolbar is on the screen, its name is ticked).

⇨ *You can also right-click one of the toolbars displayed and click the name of the bar you wish to show or hide.*

B- Moving a toolbar

▷ Point to the bar's move handle ⠿ and drag it to its new position.

drag the title bar to move a "floating" toolbar

▷ To dock a floating toolbar, double-click its title bar.

C- Customising a toolbar

Opening the Rearrange Commands dialog box

> Make sure the toolbar that you want to modify is displayed in the application window.
> **View - Toolbars - Customize** or **Tools - Customize**
> In the **Customize** dialog box, click the **Commands** tab if necessary.
> Click the **Rearrange Commands** button.

Removing a tool button

└ click to retrieve the original toolbar

|1| Activate this option.

|2| Select the toolbar that contains the item you wish to remove: only the bars that are currently visible on the screen are noted in this list.

|3| Click the name of the tool that you wish to remove.

|4| Click to remove the tool button.

▷ Close the **Rearrange Commands** and **Customize** dialog boxes.

⇨ You can use the same technique to remove a menu or menu option, taking care to activate the **Menu Bar** option so you can choose which item you wish to remove.

⇨ Another way to remove a tool button, menu or menu option is to open the **Customize** dialog box, select the item concerned on its bar or in the menus and drag it clear of the toolbars and menus.

Adding a tool button

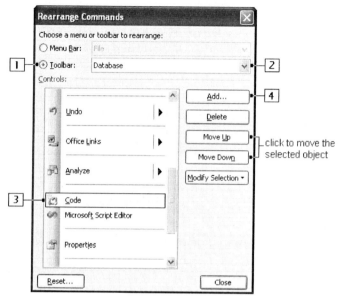

1 Activate this option.

2 Select the toolbar to which you wish to add an item: only the bars that are currently visible on the screen are noted in this list.

3 Choose the item above which the new element should appear.

4 Click the **Add** button.

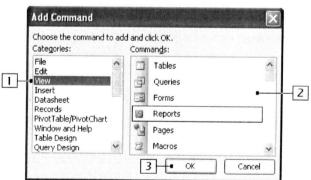

1 Select the required options category.

2 Click the name of the command that you want to add.

3 Click to confirm.

▷ Click the **Close** button on the **Rearrange Commands** and **Customize** dialog boxes.

The command (**Reports** in this example) is added to the toolbar (here, in the middle of the **Database** toolbar, between the **Spelling** and **Print Preview** buttons).

⇒ You can use the same technique to add a menu or menu option, by following these guidelines:
- to add a menu, select **Menu Bar** in the **Toolbar** list in the **Rearrange Commands** dialog box. In the **Categories** list in the **Add Command** dialog box, choose **New Menu** or **Built-in Menus**, depending on what you want to add.
- to add a menu option, activate the **Menu Bar** option, select the menu or submenu concerned in the list of commands and proceed as if you were adding a tool button.

⇒ You can also show hidden buttons or hide buttons on an open toolbar by clicking the black triangle on almost any toolbar's right, and choosing the **Add or Remove Buttons** option.

⇒ Another way to add a tool button, menu or menu option is to open the **Customize** dialog box at the **Commands** tab, select one of the **Categories**, then one of the **Commands** and drag the selected command onto the bar or menu in question (which must be open in the application window).

⇒ The **Modify Selection** button in the **Rearrange Commands** dialog box can be used to rename the item selected in the Controls box, or to customise its appearance. To rename the item, enter a new **Name** in the text box, putting the **&** character before the required shortcut letter, then press the ⏎Enter key.

D-Creating a custom toolbar

▷ Open the database for which you want to create a new toolbar; the new toolbar will not be available in any other database.

▷ **Tools - Customize**

▷ Click the **Toolbars** tab and then the **New** button.

▷ Enter the **Toolbar name** for your new bar and click **OK**.

▷ Add all the tool buttons you require using the **Commands** page and click the **Close** button.

To remove a custom toolbar, click the name of the toolbar in question in the **Customize** dialog box (**Tools - Customize - Toolbars** tab), click the **Delete** button then click **OK** to confirm.

2.1 Databases

A- What are the objectives of your database?

Microsoft Access 2003 is a relational database management system that works in a Windows environment. Microsoft Access is used to manage data relating to a particular subject, such as stock control, personnel records etc., while working within a single database file. In this file, related data are stored in tables and these tables are linked by a system of common fields. The links, or relationships between tables allow you to create objects (forms, queries, reports and so on) that can bring together information stored in several different tables.

Before sitting down to create your database, you should first think carefully about why you are creating it and what the aim of your database is.

▷ What information will you be managing with the database and what should you place in each table? For example, one table may contain the list of product categories, with a description, an illustration and so on; another may contain all the articles. Linking these two tables by means of a category code would allow you to work simultaneously with the product information and the category information (in a report, for example).

▷ Try to avoid repeating the same information from one table to another; in a table that lists each customer order made, it is not necessary to repeat the client information (name, address and so on), as you will have to fill in the same fields each time an order is placed (this wastes time and disk space and produces mistakes).

▷ You should also note what documents you wish to produce from the information stored, such as printed lists (products, customers etc.), statistics, charts, calculations and so on.

B- Creating a database without a wizard

▷ **File**
  New   **N**

▷ Click the **Blank database** link in the **New File** task pane.

▷ Select the folder where you want to store the database then give the database a name in the **File name** text box.

▷ Click the **Create** button.

A new database window appears on the screen.

▷ You can then create each object that will make up the database and define the relationships between the tables.

⇨ The **From existing file** link in the **New File** task pane creates a database based on an existing file. The new database contains all the objects from the file on which it is based. It is saved in the active folder and its name is the name of the file from which it was created followed by a number (e.g. MyBase1.mdb).

C- Creating a database with the Database Wizard

> **File** `Ctrl` **N**
> **New**

> Click the **On my computer** link in the **New File** task pane.

> Click the **Databases** tab, if necessary, then double-click the icon that corresponds to the type of database you wish to create.

> Select the folder where you want to store the database then give the database a name in the **File name** text box.

> Click the **Create** button then click **Next** to go to the next step in the wizard.

▷ In the **Tables in the database** list, click each table in succession and in the **Fields in the table** list, tick any extra fields (those in italics) you wish to add to the tables. Fields that are already ticked cannot be deselected as they are necessary for the construction of the chosen database.

▷ Click **Next** then choose a style for the presentation of the data entry windows (forms) in the database.

▷ Click **Next** then choose a style for the presentation of reports.

▷ Click **Next** then enter the title for the database. If you want a picture to appear on all the reports, tick the **Yes, I'd like to include a picture** option and click the **Picture** button to select one.

▷ Click **Next** then, if you wish, leave the **Yes, start the database** option active. This ensures that once the database has been created, a **Main Switchboard** window appears on the screen. When this happens, the database window is minimized to an icon and you simply click one of the switchboard options to go to the corresponding action (adding or displaying records, viewing reports and so on). If you deactivate this option, the database window appears and you must work directly within it.

You can display the **Main Switchboard** window again at any time by clicking **Forms** in the objects bar on the database window then double-clicking the **Switchboard** form.

▷ Click the **Finish** button.

▷ If the **Yes, start the database** option is not active, Access tells you when it has finished creating the database. Click **OK** to view the database window. If that option was active, the **Main Switchboard** window appears directly on the screen.

D- Opening a database

▷ **File** `Ctrl` **O**
> **Open**

You can also click the **More** link in the **Open** section of the **Getting Started** task pane.

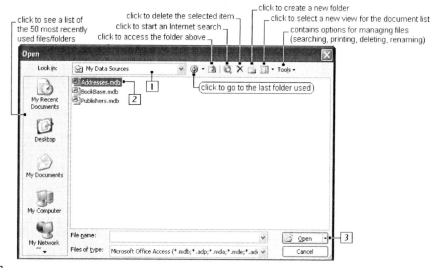

|1| Go to the required drive then double-click to open the folder containing the file.

|2| Select the name of the database file.

|3| Click this button to open the database "normally" or open the list on the button to open the database in read-only and/or exclusive mode (which prevents other users from opening it).
*The first time you open a database in the Microsoft Access application, a message opens offering to install the **Microsoft Jet 4.0 Service Pack 8** application, which can block potentially dangerous expressions, while still allowing Access to work normally.*

▷ If you want to install this application, make sure that your Internet connection is online and click the **Windows Update** link that appears in the text of the message. If you do not want to install it, click **Yes** on the security message to open the database, with the risk that the database may contain expressions that malicious users could use to damage files on your computer.

▷ Depending on the security level defined for macros (cf. Macros chapter - Setting macro security levels), you may see a message telling you that your file may contain code that could be harmful to your computer.

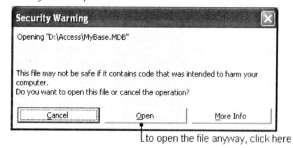

to open the file anyway, click here

The database window opens inside the Microsoft Access 2003 application window.

⇨ *A list of the last four databases that you have opened appears at the bottom of the* **File** *menu or in the* **Open** *section of the* **Getting Started** *task pane.*

⇨ *To close a database, use* **File - Close** *(Ctrl F4) or click the button on the database window.*

⇨ *Whatever the active window, you can go into the database window at any time by clicking the* *tool button.*

E- Securing a database with a password

> **File**   Ctrl O
> **Open**

▷ Go to the database you wish to secure and select it.

▷ Open the drop-down list on the **Open** button then click the **Open Exclusive** option.

▷ If necessary, click **Yes** then **Open** in the **Security Warning** dialog box.

▷ **Tools - Security - Set Database Password**

▷ Enter the password in the **Password** box, then confirm this password in the **Verify** box.

Be careful: Access differentiates between upper and lower case letters.

▷ Click **OK**.

⇨ *To remove a password, open the database in* **Exclusive** *mode then use the command* **Tools - Security - Unset Database Password**. *Type in the given password for the database then confirm with* **OK**.

F- Compacting and repairing a database

Database compression and repair are combined into a single action. Compacting a database reduces the amount of space it takes up on the disk. When you delete data and/or objects in a database, it may become fragmented, which means it takes up more space than it should. Compacting will also repair a database if it is damaged.

▷ **Tools - Database Utilities**

▷ Click the **Compact and Repair Database** option.

If a database is open, the compacting process begins immediately.

▷ If no database is open, select the database you wish to compact and click the **Compact** button.

▷ Give a name, a drive and a folder for the compacted version of the database and click the **Save** button.

⇨ *You can interrupt the compacting process by pressing* Ctrl Break *or* Esc.

⇨ *If you want a database to be compacted and repaired automatically when it is closed, activate the* **Compact on Close** *option in the* **Options** *dialog box (***Tools - Options - General** *tab).*

G-Backing up a database

You should always make a backup copy of a database.

▷ Open the database concerned, use the **Tools - Database Utilities** command then click the **Back Up Database** command.

▷ Specify where you want to save the backup copy, change the **File name** if required and click the **Save** button.

2.2 The objects within a database

A-The objects in an Access database

A database file contains a set of objects which you use to work with the data in your database.

Table   Each table in a database contains data concerning a particular subject (a list of your clients' addresses, the products distributed by your company and so on). The table is the fundamental object in the database; every query, form or report is directly or indirectly based on one or more tables.

Query   Queries are requests to extract data from one or more tables.

Form   Forms are a convenient way of entering and modifying data in a table.

Report   A report sets out data from a table with a specific presentation, so you can print that data, or even make statistical calculations or group the records.

Pages   Data access pages are web pages that you can use to add, modify or view data from a database from Access or another application, such as Excel.

Macros   A macro will save and run a series of actions automatically, such as opening a form, displaying a toolbar, etc.

Module   Module objects contain procedures developed with the Visual Basic programming language which allow you to increase the number of automated functions and event responses in Access.

B-Managing objects

▷ To see the list of all objects of a certain type, click the name of the required object type in the objects bar.

▷ To see the contents of an object, double-click the object's name or select the object and click the Type a question for help button.

▷ To see an object's structure in Design view, click the object's name then the Design button.

▷ To save an object's design, click the tool button, give the object a name, if necessary, then click **OK**.

▷ To delete an object, select it and press Del.

> To hide an object, select it, use **View - Properties**, tick the **Hidden** option and click **OK**.

> To reveal a hidden object, use **Tools - Options - View** tab, tick **Hidden objects** then click **OK**. Next, change the object's properties, deactivating the **Hidden** option.

> To rename an object, RIGHT-click the object's name, click **Rename**, enter the new name and press ⌷Enter .

▷ To copy an object, select it and use **Edit - Copy** or [icon] or ⌷Ctrl **C**. Next, go to the place where you wish to place the object and use **Edit - Paste** or [icon] or ⌷Ctrl **V**.

▷ To change the view of the list of objects, click one of the last four buttons on the **Database** toolbar: the selected view applies to all the object types (tables, reports etc.) in the database.

⇨ *If you want to be able to open an object by a simple click on its name, activate the **Single-click open** option in the **Options** dialog box (**Tools - Options - View** tab).*

C - Organizing database objects into groups

You can create shortcuts to the various types of object in a database then bring them together to form a group.

Creating a group

▷ Open the required database, then click the title of the **Groups** bar to show the groups list.

▷ Right-click the groups bar, then click the **New Group** option.

▷ Enter the **New Group Name** in the text box, then click **OK**.

*The group's icon appears in the groups bar, below the **Favorites** group which is an existing group created by Access.*

Deleting or renaming a group

▷ Open the required database then click the title of the **Groups** bar to show the groups list.

▷ Right-click the name of the group that you want to delete or rename.

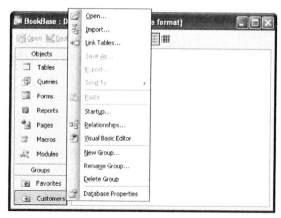

⇨ *Deleting a group also deletes all the shortcuts it contains.*

Adding an object to a group

▷ Open the required database

▷ Right-click the object that you want to add to the group and point to the **Add to Group** option.

▷ Click the name of the group to which the object shortcut should be added.

⇨ *You can also add a shortcut to a group by dragging the object concerned (form, table, etc.) onto the icon of the group to which you want to add the shortcut.*

⇨ *To rename or delete an object shortcut, right-click the shortcut in question then click the **Rename** or **Delete** option.*

D-Applying an AutoFormat to a form or report

▷ Open the form or report and display it in Design view (⟦ Design⟧), then use **Format - AutoFormat** or ⟦⟧.

▷ Click the **Options** button.

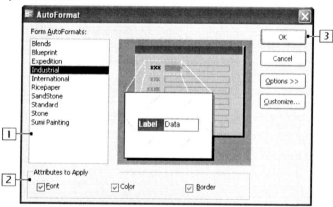

$\boxed{1}$ Select one of the formats from the list.

$\boxed{2}$ Deactivate the check box for each attribute you do not want to apply to your form or report.

$\boxed{3}$ Click to apply the format.

▷ Click the 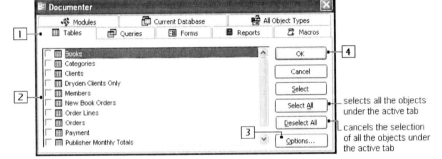 or ▢ tool button to view the result.

▷ Save the changes made to the form or report by clicking ▢ then close it if necessary.

E - Displaying the definition of an object

▷ **Tools - Analyze - Documenter**

▷ A message may appear, to tell you that the necessary component is not installed. If necessary, insert the Microsoft Office 2003 or Access 2003 CD-ROM in your drive and click the **Yes** button.

$\boxed{1}$ Activate the tab containing the objects concerned.

$\boxed{2}$ Tick the check box on each object whose definition is to be displayed.

$\boxed{3}$ Click this button to choose what you want to display.

$\boxed{4}$ Click to see the object's characteristics.

A definition of the object(s) appears as a report.

▷ Print the document, if you need to, then close the object.

F - Creating a shortcut to an object

This action creates a shortcut on the Windows desktop that you can use to open an object quickly.

▷ Select the database object concerned then use **Edit - Create Shortcut**.

▷ If the database is not on the local disk, tick the **This Database is on the Network** option and give the file path to the database.

▷ Click **OK**.

⇨ *A double-click on the shortcut on the Windows desktop opens the database then the object.*

G-Viewing object dependency information

*In an Access database, when you create a form, a report, a query or a data access page, you always need to use data from a table or query. You could say that an object uses other objects (for example, a **Client List** report uses the **Clients** table) and in turn, an object is used by other objects (for example, the **Clients** tables is used by a **Client List** report, by a **New Clients** form and by a **Recent Clients** query). Access can display for you a schema of the dependencies that exist between the objects in your database, which can save you time and help avoid errors.*

▷ So that Access can supply you with precise up-to-date information, make sure the objects are saved and closed. Open the **Options** dialog box (**Tools - Options - General** tab) and in the **Name AutoCorrect** frame, make sure the **Track name AutoCorrect info** option is active; if the **Perform name AutoCorrect** option is active, it will automatically update changes in object names. The **Log name AutoCorrect changes** option keeps a record of the changes made to object names and saves these in a **Name AutoCorrect Log** table; each change is a separate record in the table.

▷ Select the object whose dependency information you want to display, then use **View - Object Dependencies**.

Access may display a message telling you that the dependency information needs updating.

▷ Click **OK** to confirm.

*In this example, the **Object Dependencies** task pane shows the list of objects that use the **Clients** table.*

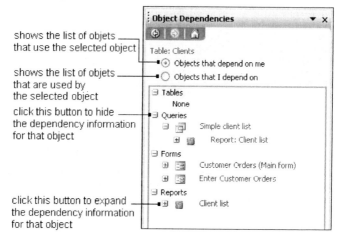

shows the list of objets that use the selected object

shows the list of objets that are used by the selected object

click this button to hide the dependency information for that object

click this button to expand the dependency information for that object

*In the example here, the dependency information about the **Simple client list** query has been expanded, so you can see that the **Client list** report uses this **Simple client list** query.*

▷ Once you have finished using the **Object Dependencies** task pane, close it by clicking its ⊠ button.

1 Table design

A-Creating a table in a database

Preparing to create a table

▷ A table is a set of data organised with a particular structure or **design**.
This design is based on one fundamental element: the **field**.
Each field in the table represents a particular category of information (a Surname field contains a list of names, a Postcode field contains postal or zip codes and so on).
Each set of fields (along with the data they contain) makes up a **record** (in a Clients table, for example, each record is the set of information referring to a single customer).
Each record in the table is designed to contain the same pieces of information, even though some records may have fields that are not filled in.
This set of data is brought together in a table, consisting of columns (the fields) and rows (the records).
Here is an example:

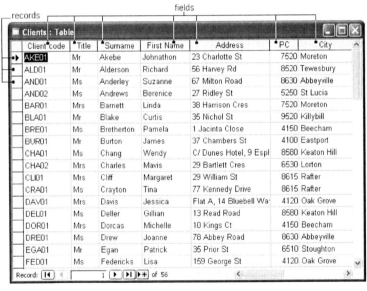

▷ In a table's design, you can name the fields on which it is based and determine the properties of those fields, such as the type of data they should contain (text, numbers, dates) and the maximum number of characters that can be entered (the field length). One of the fields in the table should give each record a unique identity. This is the **primary key** (if you do not define one, Access can do so and manage the data it contains automatically).

Creating a table with a wizard

▷ Click **Tables** in the objects bar then double-click the **Create table by using wizard** shortcut that appears in the list of tables.

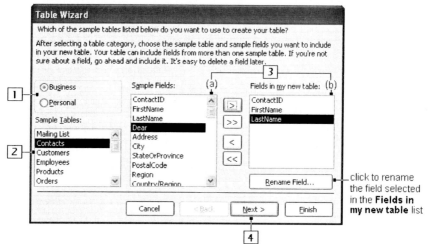

click to rename the field selected in the **Fields in my new table** list

|1| Select the type of table you wish to create.

|2| Select one of the sample tables that is closest to the table you had in mind.

|3| Indicate which fields you wish to include in the table: for each field you are inserting, select it in list (a) and click the ⟩ button; to insert all the fields in the list, click ⟩⟩; to remove a field from the list, select it in list (b) and click the ⟨ button; to remove all the fields from this list, click ⟨⟨.

|4| Click to go to the next step in the wizard.

▷ Give the table a name and indicate how the primary key is to be defined by activating one of the options.

▷ Click the **Next** button, then, if you are defining the primary key yourself, specify which field to use and the type of data it will contain.

▷ Click **Next**, then the **Relationships** button if you want to define the relationship that exists between the table you are creating and one or more existing tables.

▷ Click **Next**, then specify what you want to do next with the new table.

▷ Click the **Finish** button.

Creating a table without using a wizard

▷ Click **Tables** in the objects bar then double-click the **Create table in Design view** shortcut that appears in the list of objects.

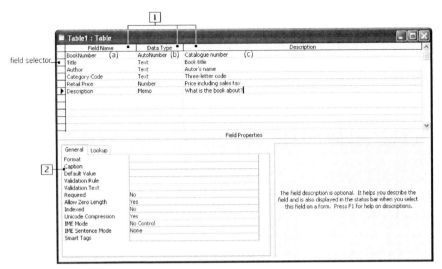

[1] For each field you want to insert in the table:

(a) enter the name of the field (use between 1 and 64 characters).

(b) give a description of the field.

(c) choose the authorised data type:

Text alphanumerical characters (letters and/or numbers); the length of a text field is limited to 255 characters.

Memo alphanumerical characters; the length of a Memo field is limited to 65535 characters.

Number any numbers, with or without decimal points.

Date/Time dates or times.

Currency the values are presented in a currency format, in accordance with your regional settings (e.g. £1,050.00 or $1,050.00).

AutoNumber a numerical value, incremented automatically when a new record is entered.

Yes/No only two items are allowed in this sort of field: Yes or No.

OLE Object this type of field is used to insert various objects made in other Windows applications into the table.

Hyperlink this type of field contains text used to make a hyperlink address.

Lookup Wizard starts a wizard that creates a field in which the field value is selected ("looked up") in a field in another table.

[2] Define the properties of each field (cf. 3.1 - C - Modifying field properties).

▷ If necessary, specify which field is to be the primary key: click the corresponding row then click the [image] tool button. To create a composite primary key (made from several fields), select the fields concerned with [Ctrl]-clicks then click the [image] tool button.

▷ Save the table's design with the **File - Save** command or [image] or [Ctrl] **S**.

▷ If required, close the table.

⇨ *The name of a table can contain up to 64 characters.*

B - Modifying a table's design

▷ Open the table in Design view ![Design].

▷ To insert a field, select the row above which you wish to insert it, press ⎣Ins⎦ or click the
![tool button] tool button. Enter the characteristics of the field.

▷ To delete a field, select the corresponding row then press ⎣Del⎦ or click the ![tool] tool
button. Click **Yes** to confirm the deletion (all the data within the field will be lost).

▷ To rename a field, select it, press the ⎣Del⎦ key then enter the new name.

▷ To move a field, click the corresponding field selector then drag the field row into its
new position.

▷ To modify the **Data Type** allowed, select the new type in the drop-down list (the data
must be convertible from one type to another).

▷ You can also modify the field properties; however, if you reduce the size of a field, make
sure that the field values can all fit in the new size.

▷ Click ![save] to save the changes made to the table's design.

▷ Close the table, if necessary.

⇨ *If a form is associated with the table, you will have to carry over the changes into the
form. However, any new forms or reports created from the table will take into account its new structure.*

⇨ *You can also modify the design of a table in Datasheet view. In this view you can
delete or move columns (fields), insert new ones or rename the existing columns (by
double-clicking the column header).*

C - Modifying field properties

*Each field has property values, which are the various characteristics that define the
field. The available properties may differ, depending on the data type of the selected
field (Text, Number, AutoNumber, Date/Time, etc).*

▷ Open the table concerned in Design view ![Design].

▷ Click the field whose properties you want to change.

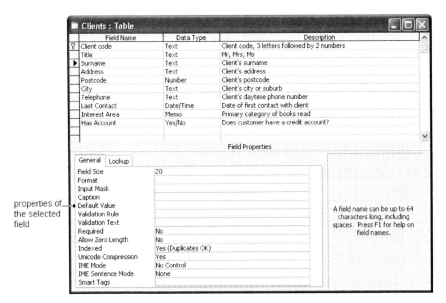

properties of the selected field

▷ Click the text box of the property in question and make your changes:

Field Size: for a Text type field, enter the number of characters that can be entered (up to 255).

For a Number type field, open the drop-down list then select the required size for the field.

Format: for Number, Currency, Date/Time or Yes/No type fields, open the drop-down list and select one of the preset formats or enter a custom format if none of the preset formats are suitable.

For Text or Memo type fields, create a custom format using special characters (for example, the ">" symbol places all the characters in upper case letters and the "<" symbol puts them all in lower case letters).

Decimal Places: for Number or Currency type fields, open the drop-down list then select the required number of decimal places for the selected field.

Input Mask: for Text, Number, Currency and Date/Time type fields, this property uses special characters to control how data can be entered in the field. You can define an input mask yourself or by using a wizard (to do this, click [...]). For example, you can create an input mask for a client code that would oblige you to enter three letters followed by three numbers (the mask would be **LLL000**: **L** means you must enter a letter and **0** means you must enter a number).

To see the list of characters that you can use to make an input mask, click the **Input Mask** property then press [F1]. When **Input Mask** and **Format** properties have been defined on the same field, the **Format** property has prevalence and the input mask is ignored.

Caption: for all field types, you can enter a text that will replace the name of the field when it is displayed in a datasheet, a form or a report.

Default Value: for all field types (except OLE Object and AutoNumber), you can specify the value that will appear automatically in the field when you enter a new record; the user can accept this value or enter another one.

Access 2003

New Values: for AutoNumber type fields; open the drop-down list then select one of the two options proposed. These options determine how the field value is incremented when a new record is added to the table.

Validation Rule: for all field types except OLE Object and AutoNumber; you can enter an expression that limits the values that can be entered in the field. For example you could create an expression for a **Title** field that would force you to enter either **Mr, Mrs** or **Miss**: in the **Validation Rule** property this expression would be **Mr or Mrs or Miss**.

Validation Text: for all field types except OLE Object and AutoNumber; enter a text that would appear in an error message if the data entered in the field did not correspond to the **Validation Rule** property. If you define the **Validation Rule** property without defining a **Validation Text**, Microsoft Access displays a standard error message when the field data does not meet the validation rule.

Required: for all field types except AutoNumber; if you want to make it compulsory to enter a value in this field when a new record is created, open the drop-down list and choose **Yes**. **No** is the default for this property.

Allow Zero Length: for Text, Memo or Hyperlink type fields; open the drop-down list and choose **Yes** if you wish to allow zero-length strings in the field (this is symbolised by " ": a zero-length string means there is deliberately no value entered in that field). The **No** option is selected by default.

Indexed: for all field types except Memo, Hyperlink and OLE Object; you can index a field by choosing **Yes (Duplicates OK)** or **Yes (No Dupli-cates)** in the drop-down list. In this case, Access will find records more quickly during a search, or when running a query or a sorting operation.

When you index a table by a field, Microsoft Access stores the values from that field "to one side", establishing a link with the records in the table. When you make a search in that field, Microsoft Access does not look in the table (which contains all the values in all the fields) but only in the list of indexed values, producing a faster result. Because the index and the table are still linked, the record corresponding to the indexed value is found rapidly. Access automatically indexes a table's primary key (no duplicates allowed).

Unicode Compression: for Text, Memo or Hyperlink type fields; if you select **Yes**, any character whose first byte equals **0** could be compressed during storage and decompressed during retrieval. This applies to all characters in Latin languages such as English, French or Spanish.

Microsoft Access uses the Unicode character coding system; in this system, each character is represented by 2 bytes. This means that Text, Memo or Hyperlink fields require more storage space than previously. Unicode compression can reduce the amount of space needed.

Smart Tags: for all field types, except Yes/No and OLE Object, click the ⸬⸬⸬ button and tick the smart tags that you want to associate with the field. Smart tags offer you rapid access to certain actions, such as sending e-mail or opening contact cards.

▷ Press ⌜Enter⌝ to confirm the new field property.

If the property you have just filled in changes the value of a field (for example, putting a Text field in uppercase or changing a date format; some properties, such as **Field Size** *do not change the field's value), then Access will display a* **Property**

Update Options 🖻 *button next to the property's name, so you can choose whether to carry this change over to form and/or report controls using the field in question.*

▷ If you want to update the property, click the 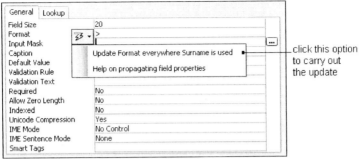 button.

This dialog box appears on the screen:

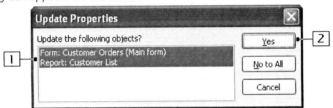

1 If necessary, click the name of each of the objects you want to update, to select them.

2 Click to make the update.

▷ Click the ▨ tool button to save the changes made to the properties.

▷ If necessary, close the table.

⇨ *Certain field properties can be modified in the Design view of a query, a form or a report. When you do this, the changes apply only to that field in the current object. If you create a new object containing that field, the object will take the field properties defined in the table and not those defined previously in the design of the query, form or report.*

⇨ *To read the help text concerning a particular property, click the property and press* F1 .

D-Creating a lookup column

In a lookup column you can select the values you need instead of typing them in. The values used for this type of field can either be defined when you create the field or can be looked up in another table or query (hence the name of this type of field!).

Using a list of fixed values

You need to state what values will be available in the list.

▷ Display the table concerned in Design view ☑ Design .

▷ Enter the **Field Name** in the corresponding column or click its row if it already exists.

▷ Open the list on the field's **Data Type** column, then select the **Lookup Wizard** option.

▷ Activate the **I will type in the values that I want** option then click the **Next** button.

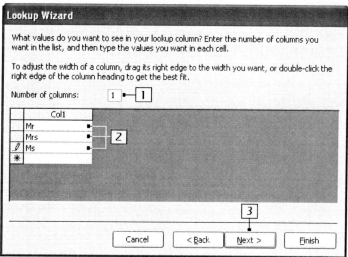

1 | Give the number of columns required for the list.

2 | Enter the values for the list as in a datasheet: the ⬚ key takes you to the next cell.

3 | Click to go to the next step.

▷ If necessary, choose the name of the column that contains the value you wish to store or use in your database.

This step occurs only if you specify more than 1 column in the previous step.

▷ Click **Next** and enter the text for the field label in the text box.

▷ Click the **Finish** button.

*To view the lookup column's properties, click the **Lookup** tab in the lower part of the window.*

▷ Save the changes made to the table and close it if necessary.

⇨ *A lookup column control can also be created for a form in Design view, using the ⬚ or ⬚ tool in the toolbox.*

Using a list of data from another table

The lookup column will contain values from a field in an existing table or query.

▷ Display the table concerned in Design view ✏ Design

▷ Enter the **Field Name** in the corresponding column or click its row if it already exists.

▷ Open the list on the field's **Data Type** column, then select the **Lookup Wizard** option.

▷ Make sure the first option is active then click the **Next** button.

▷ In the list, select the table or query that contains the values you wish to insert then click the **Next** button.

▷ Select the field(s) whose values should appear in the lookup column then click the **Next** button.

▷ Specify a sort order for the list: the **Ascending** button indicates an ascending order and the **Descending** button, a descending order.

▷ Click the **Next** button.

▷ Deactivate the **Hide key column (recommended)** option if you want to see the column containing the primary key values, modify the width of the list's columns (if necessary) then click the **Next** button.

▷ Select the field in which you wish to store the value then click **Next**.

*This step occurs only if the **Hide key column** option is deactivated.*

▷ Enter the text for the lookup column's label then click the **Finish** button.

▷ To view the lookup column's properties, click the **Lookup** tab in the lower part of the window.

Had you not used the wizard, you would have had to define these options yourself:

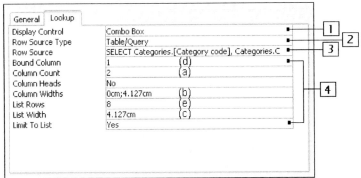

1 The type of list.

2 The data source.

3 The name of the table or query containing the field values or the SQL statement that selects the values you want to insert in the list. If only one table or query name is given, the columns in the list will contain the values from the x first fields in the table/query, with x being the number of columns.

4 The number of columns (a), their respective widths (b) and the total width of the list (c). The column number that contains the field used for table linking (d) as well as the numbers of rows visible in the list (e).

▷ Save the changes made to the table and close it if required.

⇨ *A lookup column control can also be created for a form in Design view, using the* ▣ *or* ▣ *tool in the toolbox.*

TABLES

E - Indexing a table

Creating a single-field index

▷ Open the table concerned in Design view.

▷ Click the row of the field on which you want to base the index and modify the value in the **Indexed** property.

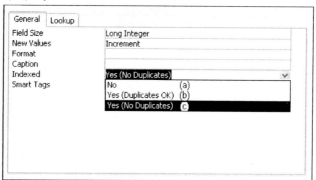

(a)   Access will not index the field.

(b)   Access indexes the field and accepts duplicate values within it.

(c)   Access indexes the field but does not accept any value which already appears in that field (the primary key is indexed in this way).

▷ Click the 🖫 tool button to save the changes made to the table, then close the table if you wish.

Creating a multiple-field index

▷ Open the table in Design view.

▷ To create an index based on more than one field, click the tool button to display the **Indexes** window.

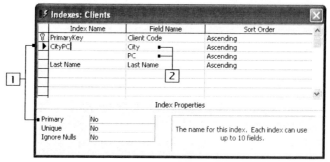

1 Give the index name and the associated properties:

Primary   choose this to make the current index the table's primary key.

Unique   choose this property if the values in the field must be unique.

Ignore Nulls   if the field is likely to remain blank for a large number of records, activate this option to speed up use of the index.

2 | Define the field(s) that will make up the index (up to 10 fields).

▷ Click the ❌ button on the window or the 📝 tool button to close the **Indexes** window.

▷ Click the 💾 tool button to save the changes made to the table, then close the table if necessary.

⇨ Although creating an index speeds up searching and sorting, it slows down data update (when you edit data, the index must be updated).

F- Defining a primary key

Each table in a database should include a field or set of fields that give each record a unique identity: this is called the **primary key**.

▷ Open the table concerned in Design view.

▷ If the primary key is to use a single field, select the corresponding row. If the primary key uses several fields, select the rows that correspond to the various fields (use the Ctrl key if the rows are not adjacent).

A primary key can be made up of more than one field when you cannot ensure that the values in a single field will all be different.

▷ Click the 🔑 tool button.

A key symbol appears on each selected row.

▷ Click the 💾 tool button to save the changes made to the table, then, if necessary close the table.

.2 Table relationships

A- Establishing a relationship between two tables

Different types of relationships between tables

Creating a relationship between tables in your database allows you to analyse, at one glance, data stored in different places, and to use that data more efficiently. Tables are joined by the primary key of one of them. Between two tables, three types of relationship are possible, which are created and managed differently:

- The **"one-to-many"** relationship: a record in the primary table can have several matching records in the related table (the primary table contains the primary key by which the tables are joined). For example, each Category code is matched with many Item codes (many arrows "leave from" a single Category code), but each Item code is matched with just one Category code.

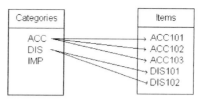

- The **"many-to-one"** relationship is the same sort of relationship but in reverse (the direction depends on the primary table). For example, an order number can match only one client, but the same client code can appear in several orders.

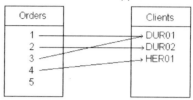

- In a **"many-to-many"** relationship, a record in the primary table can match many records in the related table, and a record in the related table can correspond to many records in the primary table. For example, one order number matches several item codes, and one item code has several corresponding order numbers.

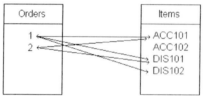

To manage this type of relationship correctly, you should split it into a "one-to-many" relationship, and a "many-to-one" relationship, by creating an intermediate table:

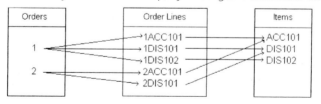

- The **"one-to-one"** relationship: one record in the primary table matches a single record in the related table, and vice-versa. This type of relationship is rare as the two tables would ordinarily be combined into a single table. The only circumstance where you might meet this type of relationship is when the related table contains temporary data to be deleted later (it is easier to delete a superfluous table than to delete a few fields from an all-inclusive table).

Establishing a relationship between two tables

You must relate the tables by the primary key field of the primary table, and the corresponding field in the related table. Tables can be related providing they have a field in common (even if its name is not the same in the two tables).

▷ If you are in the database window, use the **Tools - Relationships** command or click the ⊞ tool button.

*When you go into the **Relationships** window for the first time in the active database, the window is empty and Access prompts you to add tables to it.*

▷ Select the tables between which you wish to create relationships (use 🔲Shift -clicks or Ctrl -clicks if necessary). Click the **Add** button.

▷ When all the necessary tables have been added, click the **Close** button.

The tables appear in the window but as yet no relationships have been established.

▷ To establish a relationship between the tables, drag the field which is common to both from the primary table towards the related table.

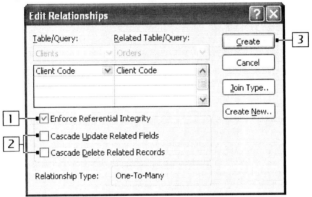

You define the relationship's attributes in the dialog box illustrated above.

1 Activate this option if you want Access to ensure the compatibility of the data in the two tables. It does this by checking that corresponding data exists in the primary table every time you add a record to the related table, and by refusing to delete a record from the primary table if it has one or more matched records in the related table.

2 Even if you have activated the referential integrity option, you can still modify the primary key, or delete records from the primary table, provided you activate these option(s). In the first case, Access will update all the related records so that they take account of the changes in the primary key; in the second, Access deletes any record related to the one you deleted.

3 Click to create the relationship.

TABLES

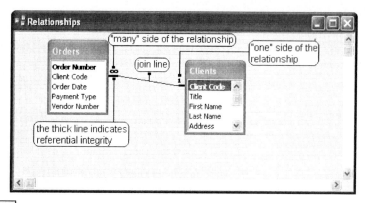

▷ Click 🖫 to save the relationship you have defined.

▷ Click the ❎ button on the **Relationships** window to close it.

▷ To see the contents of the **Relationships** window again, click the ⊞ tool button.

⇒ It is not possible to delete a primary table, or to change the data type of a field used in a join, or to delete such a field.

⇒ You can establish only one relationship between the same two tables.

B- Managing relationships in a database

▷ If you are in the database window, click the ⊞ tool button to open the **Rela-tionships** window.

If the **Relationships** window is empty, Access prompts you to add tables or queries.

▷ To add one or more tables to the **Relationships** window, use the ⊞ tool button, select the tables, click the **Add** button then click **Close**.

▷ To remove one of the tables from the window, click its title bar then use the **Rela-tionships - Hide Table** command (or press Del). To clear the entire contents of the window, use the **Edit - Clear Layout** command.

Be careful, simply removing a table from the relationships window does not delete its relationships with other tables.

▷ To move a table, drag the title bar of the table in question to its new position.

▷ To go into the design of a table, right-click the table concerned and choose the **Table Design** option.

▷ If you wish to edit the relationship characteristics, double-click the join line then make the required changes and click **OK**.

▷ To delete a relationship, click the join line once then press the Del key and confirm the deletion by clicking **OK**.

▷ To print the relationships as a report, use **File - Print Relationships**.

C - Showing/modifying linked data in a subdatasheet

*When two tables are linked by a **one-to-many relationship**, the rows from the table on the "many" side can be seen in a subdatasheet for each corresponding row in the table on the "one" side.*

▷ Open the table concerned in Datasheet view.

In the column to the left of each row a plus (+) sign appears.

▷ To show (and if you wish, modify) the linked data for one or more rows (records), click the + sign for the row(s) concerned.

click to hide the linked data

	Client code	Title	Surname	First Name	Address	PC	City	Telephone	Cor
▶ +	AKE01	Mr	Akebe	Johnathon	23 Charlotte St	7520	Moreton	558 3361	
⊖	ALD01	Mr	Alderson	Richard	56 Harvey Rd	8520	Tewesbury	555 2563	

	Order Number	Order Date	Payment Type
+	1	01/07/2004	CH
+	47	09/07/2004	CS
＊	(AutoNumber)		

	Client code	Title	Surname	First Name	Address	PC	City	Telephone	Cor
+	AND01	Ms	Anderley	Suzanne	67 Milton Road	8630	Abbeyville	556 1245	
+	AND02	Ms	Andrews	Berenice	27 Ridley St	5250	St Lucia	555 9986	
+	BAR01	Mrs	Barnett	Linda	38 Harrison Cres	7520	Moreton	551 1235	
+	BLA01	Mr	Blake	Curtis	35 Nichol St	9520	Killybill	551 1447	
+	BRE01	Ms	Bretherton	Pamela	1 Jacinta Close	4150	Beecham	551 2269	
+	BUR01	Mr	Burton	James	37 Chambers St	4100	Eastport	555 4411	
+	CHA01	Ms	Chang	Wendy	C/ Dunes Hotel, 9 Espl	8580	Keaton Hill	556 6990	
+	CHA02	Mrs	Charles	Mavis	29 Bartlett Cres	6530	Lorton	556 2247	

Record: ◀◀ ◀ 1 ▶ ▶▶ ▶＊ of 56

4.1 Records

A - Entering records in a datasheet

▷ To enter records in a table's datasheet, double-click the name of the table to which you wish to add new records.
To enter records in a form's datasheet, double-click the name of the form you wish to use to add new records.
Open the drop-down list on the ![tool button] tool button and choose **Datasheet View**.

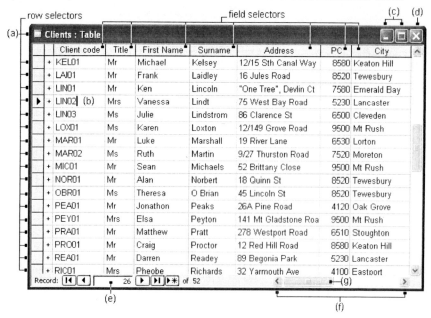

(a)	Control menu	(e)	number of current record
(b)	insertion point	(f)	scroll arrows
(c)	Minimize and Maximize buttons	(g)	scroll cursor
(d)	Close button		

▷ Click the ![▶*] button at the bottom left of the window or the ![tool button] tool button on the toolbar to create a new record.

▷ Fill in each field in the record and confirm with Enter or press ![⇄] to go to the next field or the next record.

▷ Each field in the record is entered in the same way. If you press Esc you delete the contents of the last field entered in the current record. If you press Esc a second time, you delete the contents of all the fields in the current record.

▷ Use the following shortcuts to insert certain field values:
Ctrl ; to insert the current time.
Alt Ctrl space to insert that field's default value.

| Ctrl | ' | to insert the value from the same field in the previous record. |
| Ctrl | Enter | to make a line break in the cell. |

▷ If required, close the datasheet when you have finished.

B - Managing the datasheet

Selecting rows or columns in a datasheet

▷ Display the table, query or form concerned in Datasheet view.

click here to select the row
click here to select the whole datasheet
click here to select the column

	Client code	Title	First Name	Surname	Address	PC	City
+	MIC01	Mr	Sean	Michaels	52 Brittany Close	9500	Mt Rush
+	NOR01	Mr	Alan	Norbert	18 Quinn St	8520	Tewesbury
+	OBR01	Ms	Theresa	O Brian	45 Lincoln St	8520	Tewesbury
+	PEA01	Mr	Jonathon	Peaks	26A Pine Road	4120	Oak Grove
+	PEY01	Mrs	Elsa	Peyton	141 Mt Gladstone Roa	9500	Mt Rush
+	PRA01	Mr	Matthew	Pratt	278 Westport Road	6510	Stoughton
+	PRO01	Mr	Craig	Proctor	12 Red Hill Road	8580	Keaton Hill

▷ To select a group of rows or columns, drag over their headers.

⇨ To cancel the selection, click elsewhere in the datasheet.

Modifying the column width/row height

▷ Display the table, query or form concerned in Datasheet view.
▷ Select the columns or rows concerned, if not already selected.

drag, or double-click (to fit the column to the size of its contents)

Clients : Table

	Client code	Title	First Name	Surname	Address	City	PC	Telephon
+	PEA01	Mr	Jonathon	Peaks	26A Pine Road	Oak Grove	4120	551 4472
+	PEY01	Mrs	Elsa	Peyton	141 Mt Gladsto	Mt Rush	9500	551 9465
+	PRA01	Mr	Matthew	Pratt	278 Westport F	Stoughton	6510	555 8452
+	PRO01	Mr	Craig	Proctor	12 Red Hill Roa	Keaton Hil	8580	556 6002
+	REA01	Mr	Darren	Readey	89 Begonia Par	Lancaster	5230	558 1113
+	RIC01	Mrs	Pheobe	Richards	32 Yarmouth A	Eastport	4100	555 3625
+	ROW01	Mrs	Melissa	Rowe	265 Ash Drive	Mt Rush	9500	551 8123
+	ROW02	Mrs	Mary	Rowland	254 Mt Barker I	Keaton Hil	8580	556 2215
+	SAL01	Ms	Helen	Salakis	85 Kessler Ave	Cleveden	6550	555 1184

Record: [◄◄] ◄ [　　1　] [►][►►][►*] of 52

⇨ You cannot have varying row heights in the one datasheet. As soon as you modify the height of one row (or a selection of rows), the height of all the rows in the datasheet is adjusted automatically.

⇨ You can also modify the row height/column width by using the **Row Height** and **Column Width** commands in the **Format** menu.

Freezing columns

Frozen columns remain on the screen while you scroll through other columns further away.

▷ Display the table, query or form concerned in Datasheet view.

▷ Select the columns you wish to freeze, then use **Format - Freeze Columns**.

▷ You can cancel this layout with the **Format - Unfreeze All Columns** command.

⇨ *Frozen columns will also appear on every printed page if the width of the printout is larger than the physical width of the paper.*

Hiding/showing certain columns

▷ Display the table, query or form concerned in Datasheet view.

▷ **Format - Unhide Columns**

▷ Tick or deactivate the check box for any column you wish to show or hide (ticked columns are visible).

⇨ *You can hide a single column by clicking a cell in it and using the **Format - Hide Columns** command.*

Moving a column

▷ Display the table, query or form concerned in Datasheet view.

▷ Select the column concerned.

▷ Click the field selector of the selected column and drag the column until the thick vertical line that appears is in the correct position.

Saving the presentation of a table, query or form

▷ Display the table, query or form in Datasheet view.

▷ Make your required changes to the presentation of the table (positions, height, width etc.) then use **File - Save** or ⊞ or ⌈Ctrl⌉ **S**.

▷ Close the table, query or form.

⇨ *The **Format - Font** command can be used to change the character font visible in the datasheet.*

C - Entering records with a form

▷ Open the form by double-clicking its icon.

*The form opens and in it you can see one record. The active view is **Form View** and it is in this view that you will enter the new records.*

▷ Click the ▶✱ button in the bottom left corner of the form window or ⊡ on the toolbar.

A blank form appears on the screen.

▷ For each field in the record enter the required data then press the [Enter] or [⏎] key to go to the next field or to the next record.

▷ Each field in the record is entered in the same way. If you press [Esc] you delete the contents of the last field entered in the current record. If you press [Esc] a second time, you delete the contents of all the fields in the current record.

▷ As when entering records in a datasheet, you can use shortcut keys to insert certain field values (cf. 4.1 - A - Entering records in a datasheet).

▷ Close the form window if necessary.

D-Entering different types of data

▷ When entering data, use only the type of data allowed for that field and respect the field length as well as the following rules:

- when entering a number with decimal points, use the decimal point defined in the Windows **Control Panel** (usually a full stop),

- when you fill in a Currency field, type in the field value without any formatting.

- when entering a date or time, use the format defined in the Windows **Control Panel**,

- when filling in a Memo field, you can use [⇧ Shift] [F2] to view the entire text entered.

- you cannot fill in an AutoNumber type field as the corresponding number is automatically incremented by Access,

- when filling in a Yes/No field, click the check box for **Yes** or remove the tick for **No** (you can also do this by pressing the [space] key).

- the contents of an OLE Object field cannot be entered on the keyboard as this field contains only objects inserted into the database.

- a hyperlink address can be made up of 4 parts, separated by a hash symbol: displaytext#address#subaddress#screentip. The first item is optional and corresponds to the text shown in a field or control. The second item corresponds to a full URL address or a UNC path to a document. The subaddress item refers to a location in the page or the file (such as a bookmark in a Word document or a slide number in a PowerPoint presentation). The screentip is the text that you see when you point to the hyperlink.

You can also enter this type of field using **Insert - Hyperlink** or or [Ctrl] **K**.

E- Adding records

With this technique, only the new records added are visible.

▷ In Form or Datasheet view, use **Records - Data Entry**.

A blank form (or row in the datasheet) appears. You can see that this record is numbered 1: only the records you are going to enter are currently available.

▷ Enter the new records.

▷ To show all the records again, use the **Records - Remove Filter/Sort** command.

▷ Close the table or form if necessary.

F- Moving within the records

Going to records/fields/data in Datasheet view

▷ Open the table, query or form concerned in Datasheet view (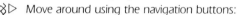).

⊘▷ Move around using the navigation buttons:

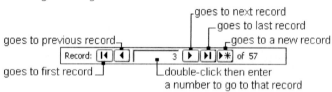

You can also slide the cursor on the vertical scroll bar until the number of the record required can be seen.

▷ To go to a given record, click its row.

▷ To select a piece of visible data (a word, a string of characters etc.) within a field, use the usual Windows selection techniques (double-click a word to select it, and so on).

▷ To select a whole field value, point to the vertical line to the left of the value and when the pointer takes the form of a thick white cross, click. Drag if you need to spread out the selection.

Ⓐ ▷ Use the following keys:

This key	Is used for
⬇/⬆	to go to the next/previous record.
Ctrl End / Ctrl Home	to go to the last field in the last record/the first field in the first record.
→ / ← or ⇄ / ⇧ Shift ⇄	to go to the next/previous field.
End / Home	go to the last/first field of the current record.
Pg Dn / Pg Up	to show the next screen down/last screen up.
Ctrl Pg Dn / Ctrl Pg Up	to show the next screen to the right/to the left.
Ctrl ⬇ / Ctrl ⬆	to go to the same field in the last/first record.
F5	to give the number of the record to which you want to go.
F2	to select or deselect the current field (the one containing the insertion point).
Ctrl space	to select an entire column when one of its values is selected.

This key	Is used for
⇧ Shift space	to select a whole record when one of its fields is selected (⇧ Shift ↓ or ⇧ Shift ↑ can then spread the selection to the adjacent records).
Ctrl A	to select all records.

⇨ *The **Edit - Go To** command options can also be used to go to certain records.*

Going to records/fields/data in Form view

▷ Open the form concerned in Form view ( ).

▷ Use the following keys:

Pg Up / Pg Dn	to scroll up or down through the records
Ctrl End / Ctrl Home	to go to the last/first record.
↓ / ↑ or ⇄ / ⇧ Shift ⇄	to go to the next/previous field
F2	to select and deselect the current field
click the record selector	to select the record concerned
F5	prompts you to enter the number of the record you want to see
Ctrl A	to select all the records.

▷ To select visible data in a field, use the usual Windows selection techniques.

⇨ *Click elsewhere in the form to cancel a selection.*

G-Deleting records

▷ If the table or form concerned is in Datasheet view, select the rows of the records you want to delete. To delete only one record, click that row.
If the form concerned is in Form view, go to the record you want to delete.

▷ **Edit**   Ctrl -
Delete Record

▷ Click the **Yes** button to confirm deleting the record(s).

▷ If necessary, close the table or form.

⇨ *This action cannot be undone.*

⇨ *If you select the whole row of a record, you can use the Del key to delete it.*

⇨ *You can also use a query to delete in a single action all the records that meet a certain set of criteria.*

H-Sorting records rapidly

▷ Display the Datasheet view of the table, form or query containing the records you wish to sort.

▷ Click the field or one of the values in the field by which you wish to sort.

▷ Use these tool buttons: ⬛↓ to sort in ascending order, or ⬛↓ to sort in descending order.

▷ To keep the active sort order, save the table, form or query.

▷ To return to the sort order defined by the primary key, use **Records - Remove Filter/Sort**.

▷ Close the table, form or query if necessary.

⇨ *It is possible to sort by the contents of more than one column: you should select them before clicking the sort button. Access sorts first by the column the furthest to the left; when the values are identical, it sorts by the column to its right. These columns must be adjacent.*

⇨ *A complex sort order can be saved using a filter or a query.*

I- Filtering records

Filters *temporarily limit which records are displayed in a datasheet or form.*

Filtering by a single criterion

▷ Go to the form or datasheet.

▷ Click the field value by which you want to filter the records: if only part of the field value is involved, select the corresponding characters.

Records
Filter
Filter By Selection

Clients : Table

		Client code	Title	Surname	First Name	Address	PC	City	Telephone
▶	+	BAR01	Mrs	Barnett	Linda	38 Harrison Cres	7520	Moreton	551 1235
	+	MAR02	Ms	Martin	Ruth	9/27 Thurston Road	7520	Moreton	558 4235
	+	SMI01	Mr	Smithers	John	15 Tall Tree Road	7520	Moreton	558 4663
	+	STO01	Mrs	Stoke	Lynn	34 Barns Drive	7520	Moreton	558 0052
	+	AKE01	Mr	Akebe	Johnathon	23 Charlotte St	7520	Moreton	558 3361
*							0		

number of records filtered

Record: ◀◀ ◀ | 1 | ▶ ▶▶ ▶* of 5 (Filtered)

▷ To show all the records again, remove the filter by using **Records - Remove Filter/Sort** or by clicking ▽.

▷ To apply the last filter created, click the ▽ tool button again.

▷ To keep the filter, save the object by clicking 🖫: the next time you open the table, simply click the ▽ tool button to apply the filter again.

▷ Close the table, form or query if necessary.

⇨ *You can also right-click one of the field values then give the value or expression you want to use as the filter criteria in the **Filter For** text box.*

⇨ *To show all the records except those that contain the active value, use the **Records - Filter - Filter Excluding Selection** command.*

Filtering records by several criteria

▷ Open the form or datasheet.

▷ **Records**
Filter
Filter By Form

click here to see a list of the field's values

■ Books: Filter by Form						
Book Number	Title	Author	Category Code	Description	Retail Price	Number of Page
			"BIO"		<=10 ⌄	

1

2

Look for / Or /

filter design grid ⌐

1 Give the various selection criteria: Access filters the records that meet all the filter criteria simultaneously. The filter criteria can also contain operators such as $>$, $<$, $>=$, $<=$, $<>$ (unlike).

2 To filter records meeting one of several sets of criteria, click here to go to a new filter design grid. Access filters records that meet the first or second set of criteria.

▷ Click the 🇾 tool button to apply the filter.

▷ To view all the records again, remove the filter with the **Records - Remove Filter/Sort** command or 🇾.

▷ To reapply the last filter created, click the 🇾 tool button.

▷ To create another filter or modify the active filter, click the 🇾 tool button, then edit or delete the active criteria.

▷ To delete a set of criteria, click the corresponding tab then use **Edit - Delete Tab**. To delete all the sets of criteria, use **Edit - Clear Grid** or click the ✕ tool button.

▷ To save the filter, save the current object by clicking the 🖫 tool button. The next time you open the table, query or form, you can reapply the filter automatically by clicking the 🇾 tool button.

▷ To leave the filter design grid without keeping any of the changes made, click the ✕ button.

▷ Close the table, form or query, if necessary.

⇨ *A filter (as with any sort order) is associated with a database object. You can save one filter with a form and a second one with the table's datasheet. However, only one filter at a time can be associated with a particular object.*

⇨ *If you create a report or form based on a table or query which has an associated filter, the new report or form will also have the filter.*

⇨ *The **Records - Filter - Advanced Filter/Sort** command can be used to create more complex filters or sort orders, as you would in a query design grid. If you choose this command, a design grid appears (much like the one used to create queries), which will contain the criteria corresponding to the active filter.*

Access 2003

4.2 Editing data

A - Modifying a field value

▷ Open the table or form in Datasheet view [image].

▷ Use the following keys to delete characters:

Del / ←	deletes the character to the right/left of the insertion point.
Ctrl Del	deletes all the text of the field to the right of the insertion point.
Ctrl ←	deletes the word to the left of the insertion point.

▷ Use the following techniques to insert or replace text:

If you want to	Do this
Insert a new value	in Insert mode, position the insertion point as required and type the data you wish to insert.
Insert a row	press Ctrl Enter .
Activate/deactivate Insert mode	press Ins (when Insert mode is deactivated, OVR (Overtype mode) appears on the status bar).
Replace a field value by a new value	select the value (use the F2 key if you prefer) then type the new value.

▷ Close the table or form if you wish.

⇨ *The changes you make are saved automatically when you close the datasheet or form.*

⇨ *You can cancel changes made in the current record by pressing* Esc *or clicking* [image].

B - Creating a hyperlink

Creating a hyperlink to an existing file or Web page in a Hyperlink type field

▷ Open the table or query in Datasheet view, or open the form in Form view.

▷ Go to the text box of the Hyperlink type field in the record concerned.

▷ **Insert Hyperlink**   Ctrl K

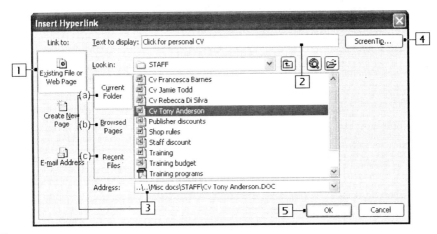

1 Activate this shortcut.

2 If necessary, enter or modify the text that should appear as the hyperlink.

3 Fill in the **Address** box, using one of these methods:

- Click this shortcut (a) then select the drive, folder and/or file to which the hyperlink will refer. If the link refers to a folder, activating the link will select the folder in the Windows Explorer.

- Click this shortcut (b) then select the page to which the link will refer.

- Click this shortcut (c) then select the file to which the link will refer.

4 If necessary, click this button then enter the text that should appear when you point to the link.

5 Click to create the hyperlink.

▷ To activate the hyperlink, simply click it.

▷ Click the tool button on the **Web** toolbar to return to the form, table or query window.

▷ Close the table, query or form if necessary.

Creating a hyperlink in a form

▷ Open the form in Design view.

▷ **Insert Hyperlink**   Ctrl K

▷ Click either the **Existing File or Web Page** or **Object in This Database** shortcut, depending on whether you want to create a link to a file, existing Web page or database object.

▷ Select the file, Web page or database object to which you want to make the link (cf. previous topic).

▷ Click **OK**.

▷ If required, move the hyperlink within the form window until it is in a satisfactory position.

Access 2003   41

▷ To activate the hyperlink, click the ▦ ▾ tool button to show the form in Form view then click the hyperlink.

▷ Click the ✖ button on the linked object's window to return to the form window.

▷ Save and close the form.

C- Finding data within records

▷ In Form or Datasheet view, click one of the field values concerned if you wish to search only in that field.

▷ **Edit**
Find

[1] Give the text you are looking for; you can make a more approximate search by including wildcard characters (* ? etc.) in your search text.

[2] Indicate whether Access should search only in the current field or in all fields on the datasheet or form.

[3] Indicate whether the text constitutes the whole value of a field, or just part of the value.

[4] Indicate the direction in which the search should be made.

[5] Start the search then click this button again to look for the next occurrence.

▷ When you find the text you were looking for, click the **Cancel** button.

▷ If Access finishes its search and does not find the specified data, a message appears: click **OK**. Close the **Find and Replace** dialog box.

▷ Close the table, query or form if necessary.

⇒ You can use the ⬆Shift F4 shortcut key to continue the last search made without having to open the **Find and Replace** dialog box again.

D-Replacing data

▷ Open the table concerned in Datasheet view.
▷ If you need to search only one field, click a value in that field.
▷ **Edit - Replace** or Ctrl **H**

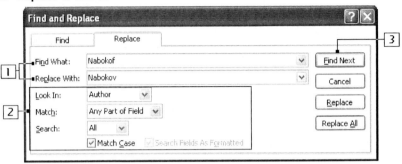

1 Enter the text you want to find and the text which will replace it.

2 Set the search options, as if you were making a search.

3 Click to start the find and replace process.

▷ If you want to make replacements one by one, click the **Replace** button to replace the selected characters and search for the next occurrence or **Find Next** to ignore that occurrence and keep searching.
To replace the text every time it occurs, click the **Replace All** button.

▷ When you have finished searching, click **OK**. If you made all the replacements at once, click **Yes** on the message telling you that you will not be able to cancel the replacements.

▷ Close the **Find and Replace** dialog box by clicking its ⊠ button.

.3 Printing data

A-Using the print preview

▷ Click the name of the table, query, form or report that you wish to preview before printing.
▷ **File - Print Preview** or 🔍

The data appear on the screen, as they will look when printed.

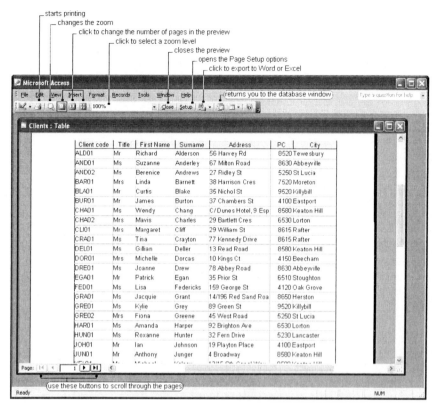

starts printing
changes the zoom
click to change the number of pages in the preview
click to select a zoom level
closes the preview
opens the Page Setup options
click to export to Word or Excel
returns you to the database window

use these buttons to scroll through the pages

⇨ *To go to a specific page, double-click the number of the active page, type the number of the page you want to see and confirm with* Enter.

⇨ *You can also show the print preview of a table or query in Datasheet view, a form in Form, Design or Datasheet view or a report in Report Design view.*

B- Changing the print margins and orientation

▷ In the database window, double-click the name of the object whose page setup you wish to edit.

▷ **File - Page Setup**

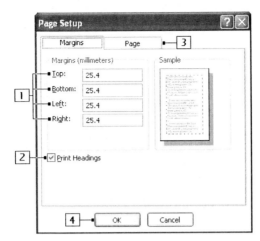

☐1 Set the margins as you require.

☐2 Tick this option if you want to print headers and footers (if not, deactivate it). For the page setup of a form or report, this option is replaced by the **Print Data Only** option, which controls printing of labels, control borders, gridlines and graphic elements.

☐3 To change the page orientation, click this tab and activate a **Portrait** or **Landscape** orientation.

☐4 Click to confirm your changes.

C- Printing a database object

▷ In the database window, double-click the name of the table, query, report or form that you want to print.

▷ If you wish, modify the page setup as required.

▷ If you want to print only certain records for a table or query, select them.

▷ **File - Print** or Ctrl **P**

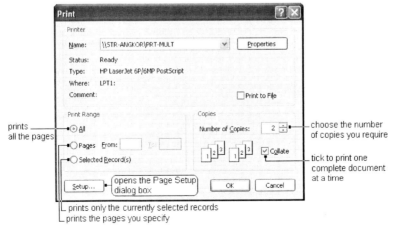

prints all the pages

choose the number of copies you require

tick to print one complete document at a time

opens the Page Setup dialog box

prints only the currently selected records
prints the pages you specify

MANAGING DATA

⇨ You can also print a table, query, report or form by selecting its name in the database window and starting to print, but this technique does not allow you to select and print certain records.

⇨ By default, Access prints the object's name and the current date in the header and the page number in the footer.

⇨ The tool button prints using the default print settings from the **Print** dialog box.

.1 Creating forms

A- Creating a form with a wizard

▷ Click **Forms** in the objects bar then click the 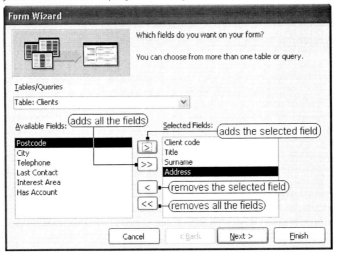 New tool button on the database window, or click **Forms** on the objects bar then click the **Create form by using wizard** shortcut, or select the table or query for which you want to create a form, open the drop-down list on the **New Object** tool button ▼, then click the **Form** option (or select the table or query and use the **Insert - Form** command).

The **New Form** *dialog box does not appear if you choose the* **Create form by using wizard** *shortcut.*

▷ Click the **Form Wizard** option.

▷ If necessary, select the table or query for which you want to create a form, and click **OK**.

Form Wizard

Which fields do you want on your form?

You can choose from more than one table or query.

Tables/Queries

Table: Clients

Available Fields: (adds all the fields)   Selected Fields: (adds the selected field)

Postcode
City
Telephone
Last Contact
Interest Area
Has Account

> Client code
>> Title
Surname
Address

< (removes the selected field)
<< (removes all the fields)

Cancel   < Back   Next >   Finish

▷ If you are using the **Create form by using wizard** technique, select the table or query on which the form is based from the **Tables/Queries** list.

▷ Specify which fields from the table should be inserted in the form (cf. illustration above) and click **Next**.

▷ Choose the type of layout you want the fields in the form to have and click **Next**.

▷ Choose a style for your form and click **Next**.

▷ Give the text that should appear on the form's title bar.

The form will also be saved under this title.

▷ Choose the first option if you wish to view the records immediately through the created form (in Form view) or the second if you wish to see the form's structure or design (Design view), then click **Finish**.

▷ To show a form in Design view, in order to modify its structure, click the tool button.

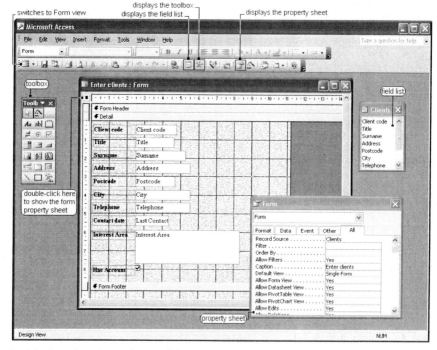

By default, a form is made up of three sections:
- the **Form Header**,
- the **Detail** section,
- the **Form Footer**.

Each element inserted in a form is called a control; for example, the form's title and the various labels shown are all controls.

When you insert a field into a form, Access draws two controls: a **field label** which contains a text that you can modify or delete (initially the name of the field) and a **text box** that displays the field value in Form view.

There are three types of control available:
- **unbound controls**, which show information that is independent from the source table or query (for example, a text you have entered into the form or a drawing object such as a rectangle or line),
- **bound controls**, which are linked to a field in the source table/query and which generally display the corresponding field value,
- **calculated controls**, which show data calculated from one or more field values using an expression that you create. For example, in a Products form, a Retail Price control might show a value calculated from the article's price plus sales tax.

▷ Close the form if necessary.

⇨ A form's source can be seen on the **Data** page of its property sheet: you can modify the **Record Source** property to change the table or query used by the form (although the two tables/queries must have a similar design); the 🔲 button on the **Record Source** row takes you to the source query.

⇨ To create an AutoForm (with predefined layout and content), select the required source table or query then use **Insert - AutoForm**.

⇨ To adapt the size of the window to fit the form, click the 🔲 ▾ tool button to go into Form view then use the **Window - Size to Fit Form** command. This command is unavailable when you display the form window full screen.

B - Setting a form's tab order

This technique sets the tab order of a form. This is the order in which fields are accessed when you press the ⇄ or Enter key while using the form.

▷ Display the form in Design view.

▷ **View - Tab Order**

field selectors

applies an order following how fields are physically placed on the form

1 │ Select the option corresponding to the appropriate section of the form.

2 │ Check the order in which the fields will be accessed, defined from top to bottom and from left to right. To move a field, select the field by clicking its field selector, then drag the field to the required position.

3 │ Click to confirm the defined order.

▷ If necessary, click the 🔲 ▾ tool button to go to Form view and see the result.

▷ Save your changes then, if required, close the form.

C-Inserting a subform

Subforms are used to display simultaneously the data from two tables that are linked by a "one-to-many" relationship. The main form represents the "one" side of the relationship and the subform represents the "many" side. The subform can appear as a datasheet or as a classic form. In the example below, the subform shows the books that each client has ordered:

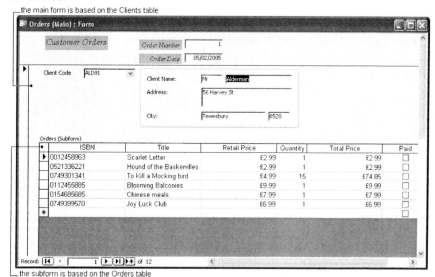

▷ Create the subform as any other form and show it in Design view.

If the subform needs to use field values from several tables, first make a query to bring together those fields, then choose that query as the subform's source.

▷ Display the subform's property sheet.

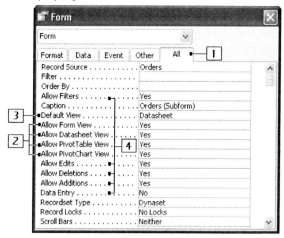

1 Click this tab.

2 Choose what views the subform can be displayed in.

3 Select the view you want to apply by default to the subform when it is opened (the **Continuous Forms** option uses a form layout but the form displays as many records at once as its size allows, while **Single Form** uses a standard one-record-per-form display).

4 Use these five properties to determine how you wish to use the form.

▷ Save the subform then close it.

▷ Open the main form in Design view.

▷ Simultaneously display the form and database windows using the **Window - Tile Horizontally** or **Tile Vertically** command:

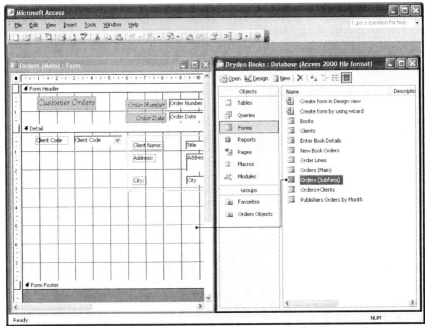

▷ Drag the subform's icon from the database window to the **Detail** section in the main form window.

Access inserts a control with the same name as the subform.

*The **Subform** can be seen inside that control.*

▷ Use the **Window - Cascade** command to overlap the two windows again and if you need to, modify the size of the main form window.

▷ If it is not selected, click the subform (black squares called selection handles appear around the edge of the control) then click 🖳 to show the subform property sheet.

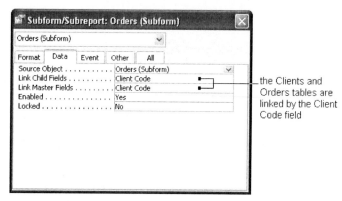

the Clients and Orders tables are linked by the Client Code field

▷ Check the **Link Child Fields** and **Link Master Fields** properties. The child field is the linking field in the subform and the master field is the linking field in the main form.

Access sets these two elements automatically when a relationship exists between the two tables, or failing that, if the two tables have a field with the same name and identical data. However, if the main form is based on a query, you have to define the **Link Child Fields** *and* **Link Master Fields** *properties yourself. If one of the two forms is based on a query, the query must contain the linking field (the child field in the subform or the master field in the main form) although that field need not necessarily be visible in the form.*

▷ If necessary, move the subform control and/or change its size.

▷ Make any necessary changes to the design of the subform. To do this, click the subform and use **View - Subform in New Window**. Make your changes, save the new design of the subform ( ) and close it.

▷ Click the tool button to view the result.

▷ Save the form then, if required, close it.

⇒ *You can use the same technique to create subreports within a main report.*

D-Inserting fields from several tables

▷ Fields from more than one table or query can be inserted into the same form or report. There are two ways of doing this:

- You can create a query in which you define a relationship between the various tables. In the Design view of the form or report, you indicate that the query is the source of that object.

- You can use the Form Wizard or Report Wizard to create your document. If you use this technique, the source of the object is not the name of the query, but rather an SQL statement created by Access so that it can find the data to display in the form or report. This SQL statement can be created by Access by means of the Query Builder: to go into it, click the button next to the form or report's **Record Source** property.

▷ Creating a query yourself is justified in two cases:

- if the query contains an expression which you want to exploit in other forms or reports,

- if you have to define criteria for filtering the records exploited by the form or the report, and if the same criteria are going to be defined for other forms or reports.

⇨ *To join two tables inserted in a query, the procedure is the same as in the **Relationships** window. The join established in the query is not visible in the **Relationships** window.*

E- Protecting a field against unauthorised access/editing

▷ With the form in Design view, click the field concerned, show its properties and click the **Data** tab.

▷ To prohibit access to a field, activate the **No** option on the **Enabled** property.

▷ To prevent a field from being modified, activate the **Yes** option on the **Locked** property.

▷ Save your changes to the form then click [⊞ ▾] to view the result.

▷ Close the form, if necessary.

⇨ *By default the text box of a calculated field is locked.*

F- Defining an input mask

▷ Open the form in Design view, click the field concerned, show its properties, then click the **Input Mask** property on the **Data** tab.

▷ Type in the value of the input mask, or click [···] to activate the **Input Mask Wizard**.

*Access may prompt you to install the **Input Mask Wizard** at this point: click **Yes** and follow the installation instructions.*

▷ If you are using the Input Mask Wizard, create the mask by following the instructions.

▷ Save the changes made to the form, then close it.

⇨ *In the property sheet, the input mask can be made up of three parts, each separated by a semi-colon.*

5.2 Creating a report

A- Creating a report with a wizard

▷ Click **Reports** on the objects bar then click the **New** button on the database window, or click **Reports** on the objects bar then click the **Create report by using wizard** shortcut, or select the table or query on which you want to base your report, open the list on the **New Object** tool button 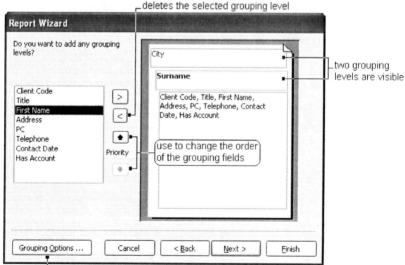 and click the **Report** option, or select the object and use **Insert - Report**.

*The **New Report** dialog box does not appear if you use the **Create report by using wizard** shortcut.*

▷ Click the **Report Wizard** option.

▷ If necessary, choose the table or query for which you wish to create a report and click **OK**.

▷ If you used the **Create report by using wizard** shortcut, select the table or query on which your report will be based, from the **Tables/Queries** list.

▷ Specify which fields you wish to include in the report and click **Next**.

▷ If you wish to group certain records in the report, select the field by which you wish to group then click the ⟩ button.

▷ Click the **Next** button.

▷ Give the sort order that should be used when the records are printed, and click **Next**.

▷ Specify how Access should lay out the fields using the **Layout** options, select the required page **Orientation** then if necessary, tick the **Adjust the field width** option to print each record on a single line.

▷ Click **Next**, then choose the style you want for your report.

▷ Click **Next** then type the text that should appear in the report's title bar. This is also the name under which the report will be saved.

▷ Activate **Preview the report** to see the result or **Modify the report's design** to go into Design view.

▷ Click the **Finish** button.

▷ Scroll through the pages of the preview using the buttons in the bottom left corner of the window.

▷ If you wish to change the structure of your report, click 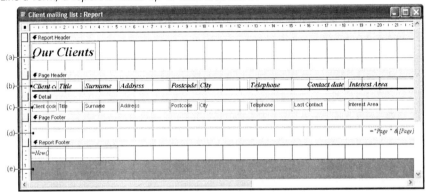 to go into Design view.

Like a form, a report is made up of several sections:

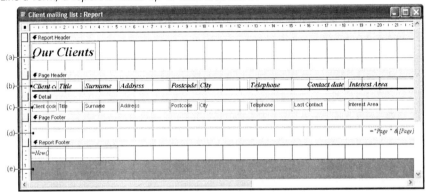

- the **Report Header** (a) contains data that will print only at the start of the first page of the report,

- the **Page Header** (b) contains the data that will print at the start of each page (the column headings for example),

- the **Detail** (c) section contains the data printed for each record (this generally consists of the text boxes for each field),

- the **Page Footer** (d) contains the data that will print at the bottom of each page. You can use the Now() function to obtain the day's date and the Page() function to insert automatic page numbering.

- finally, the **Report Footer** (e) is reserved for data that will appear on the last page of the report, after all the records.

As with a form, several different types of control can be found within a report's design (bound, unbound and calculated controls).

▷ Save the changes you made to the report's design then close it.

⇨ *The width of the report should not be greater than that of the paper used for printing (minus the set printing margins).*

⇨ *You can modify a report's presentation by using the **Format - AutoFormat** command or* ▨ *then applying one of the styles offered by the wizard.*

⇨ *To show the report's properties, double-click the grey area outside of the limits of the report or click the* ⬜ *box at the intersection of the horizontal and vertical rulers.*

⇨ *If you want the report to contain fields from several tables, there are two possibilities: you can base the report on a query in which the various tables are linked or, if you create the report with a wizard, you can select the tables and the various fields; if you do this, the report will be based on an SQL statement created by Access.*

⇨ *To create an AutoReport (with predefined layout and content), select the required source table or query then use* **Insert - AutoReport**.

B- Changing the sort order in a report

▷ Open the report in Design view.

▷ **View**
Sorting and Grouping

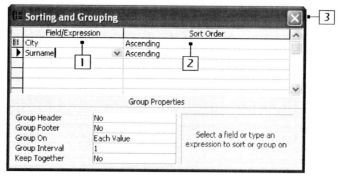

1 Select the fields you want to sort by: the first row must contain the name of the field used in the first level of sorting, the second row must contain the field used in the second level of sorting and so on.

2 For each field concerned, choose a sort order.

3 Click to close the window.

▷ Save the changes made to the report then close it.

C- Inserting subreports into a main report

This technique enables you to bring several reports together so that they can be printed all at once.

▷ Create the main report as an unbound object (the source of the report must be blank) and display it in Design view.

▷ **Window - Tile Vertically** or **Tile Horizontally**

▷ Insert each subreport into the **Detail** section of the main report by dragging the corresponding icon from the database window onto the main report window.

▷ Save the changes made to the report then close it.

D-Creating a report for printing mailing labels

▷ Click **Reports** in the objects bar then click the 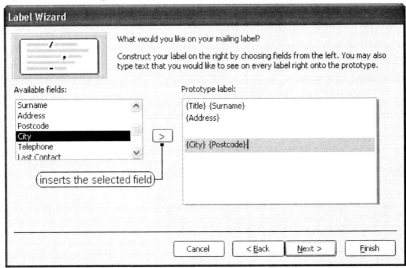 New tool button.

▷ Click the **Label Wizard** option, select the table or query for which you want to create labels and click **OK**.

▷ Select the appropriate layout for the sheet of labels and click **Next**.

▷ Set the options concerning text style then click **Next**.

▷ Indicate what you want on each mailing label by inserting fields and typing in any extra text (use Enter to change lines).

▷ Click **Next**, then select the fields by which you want to sort the labels during printing.

▷ Click **Next** to go on the next step, then enter the title for the report title bar (it will also be saved under this name).

▷ Activate the first option to see the result in a preview or the second option to go into Design view, then click the **Finish** button.

▷ If you are in the label preview, click the **Close** button to view the report in Design view.

▷ If necessary, adjust the size of the **Detail** section to fit the labels you are using for printing.

▷ Save the changes made to the report then close it.

E- Defining the page setup of labels

▷ Open the report in Design view or in Print Preview, use the **File - Page Setup** command then click the **Columns** tab.

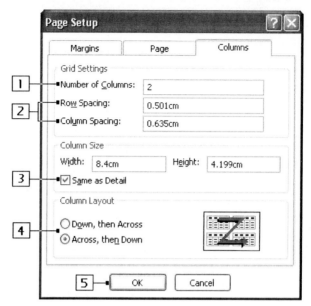

1 Give the number of labels you want to print across the width of the page.

2 If necessary, change the space left between the labels.

3 Tick this option if you want the labels to be the same size as the Detail section.

4 Give the order in which the labels should be printed.

5 Click to confirm these settings.

▷ Go into the print preview to see the end result, save the changes made then close the report.

5.3 Printing reports

A-Printing selected records as a report

Using a filter

▷ Click the **Data** tab on the report property sheet and in the **Filter** property, give the SQL statement that will extract the required records. The simplest type of SQL statement is **field name = value** (if the value is text type data, enter it between quotation marks).

▷ Activate the **Yes** option in the **Filter On** property.

▷ Save the changes made to the report, then print it.

▷ Close the report if you wish.

Using a query

▷ Click the **Data** tab on the report property sheet and in the **Record Source** property, select the name of the query you wish to use to extract certain records.

▷ Go into Print Preview and/or start to print the report to see the result.

▷ Save the report and close it, if necessary.

⇨ Of course, the query must make use of the existing fields in the report.

B- Grouping records

▷ Open the report in Design view and use the command **View - Sorting and Grouping** or 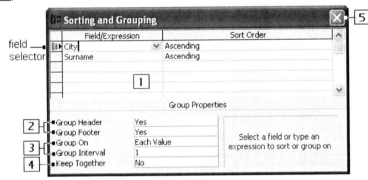.

field selector

1 Insert fields to define a sort order which will keep grouped records together.

2 For each field by which you want to group, activate these options.

3 Indicate how the records should be grouped.

4 Indicate how to deal with page breaks which may break up the group:

No　　　　　　The group of records can be split over two pages.

Whole Group　If the whole group will not fit on the current page, Access inserts a page break before it.

With First Detail　The group header cannot be printed alone at the bottom of a page: there must be room for at least one record.

5 Close the window.

▷ Define the contents of the **Group Header** and **Group Footer** sections.

▷ Preview or print the report, then save and close it.

⇨ If you use the **Report Wizard** to create your report, you can set the options for grouping during the creation process.

⇨ To print each group on a new page, open the list on the **Force New Page** property on the **Format** page of the property sheet of the section concerned and choose **Before Section, After Section** or **Before & After**.

C - Hiding the page header/footer when printing

▷ Display the report's property sheet.

▷ Define which pages should not contain the page header, using the **Page Header** option on the **Format** page.

▷ Define which pages should not contain the page footer, using the **Page Footer** option.

▷ Preview the report to see the result.

▷ Save the report then, if required, close it.

D - Hiding duplicates when printing

Duplicates are identical values which occur in the same field or record.

▷ Open the report in Design view and select the field control concerned.

▷ Show its properties then click the **Format** tab.

▷ Select **Yes** in the **Hide Duplicate** property.

▷ Save the report then, if required, close it.

.1 Bound controls

A- Inserting a text box

A text box is a bound control that displays the value of a field in a form or report.

▷ Show the design of the report or form concerned.

▷ Click the  tool button or press ⌊F8⌋ to display the field list.

▷ Drag the name of the required field from the field list onto the place on the form or report where you wish to insert it.

▷ If you do not need it, delete the accompanying label then adjust the position, size and characteristics of the text box as required.

▷ To close the window containing the field list, click the ⊠ button or deactivate the ▦ tool button.

⇨ *You can insert several fields with a single action: use* ⌊⇧Shift⌋*-clicks to select adjacent fields and* ⌊Ctrl⌋*-clicks to insert non-adjacent ones. To select all the fields, double-click the field list's title bar.*

⇨ *To insert fields from several tables, you can create a query in which you could link several tables and insert the necessary fields for your form or report. You would then, in Design view, give that query as the form or report's source.*

B- Inserting a field as a check box, an option button or a toggle button

These controls are used to manage Yes/No fields. The check box is the default presentation for a Yes/No field.

▷ Open the form/report in Design view and, in the toolbox (⚒), select the tool that you want for the control:

   check box

   option button

   toggle button

▷ Drag the **Yes/No** field concerned from the field list onto the form/report window.

▷ If you insert a toggle button, click inside it, enter the text it should display then confirm by pressing ⌊Enter⌋ .

▷ If you wish, modify the presentation of the check box, option button or toggle button.

▷ Save the changes made to the form or report then close it.

⇨ You can also place several check boxes, option buttons or toggle buttons in an option group; the user then selects one of the values displayed in that group.

⇨ You can use the **Format - Change To** command in Design view to modify the type of control used for a selected field.

⇨ The ▦ and ▤ tools can be used to create list/combo boxes in which you can select values from a list. These lists, also called lookup fields, can also be created directly in a table's design (cf. Table design - Creating a lookup column).

C- Inserting an option group into a form

The three sales vendors available in this form are presented as an option group:

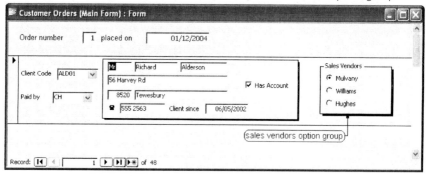

▷ With the form in Design view, make sure the ▦ tool button is active on the toolbox then click the ▦ tool button.

▷ Drag to draw the outline of the option group control.

Access starts the **Option Group Wizard**.

▷ Enter the text for each label in the option group as in a datasheet, then click **Next**.

▷ If you wish, choose the value that will be active by default from the list of labels then click **Next**.

▷ Indicate the value you wish to assign to each option in the group: these are the values that will be stored in the table.

You can create an option group only for number or AutoNumber type fields.

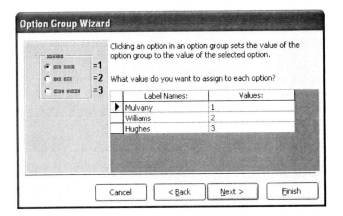

▷ Click **Next**.

▷ Activate the **Store that value in this field** option then select the corresponding field (this must be a numerical or AutoNumber field) and click **Next**.

▷ Select the type of button and the style of frame you want to use then click **Next**.

▷ Enter the text for the group label in the appropriate box then click the **Finish** button.

▷ To see the properties of the group, click ▨ then the **Data** tab. The **Option Value** property determines the value stored in the form's source table when a user chooses that button.

▷ Save the changes made then close the form.

D-Inserting an object

Inserting a bound object

*The object is linked to an **OLE Object** type field.*

OLE Object *type fields are used to insert an object made in another Windows application into a form. This application must be a **server** application, with Access being the **client** application. This result is brought about by one of two methods:*

- *by **embedding** the object. The inserted object becomes an integral part of the destination document; to modify it, you must first open that document.*
- *by **linking** the object. In this case, the object does not actually exist in the destination document; instead the document contains a linking formula that allows it to display the linked object when necessary.*

▷ Show the form in Design view, then click the ▨ tool button on the toolbox (▨).

▷ Drag to draw the outline for the bound object.

▷ Show the bound object's property sheet, click the **Data** tab, and in the **Control Source** property, choose a source for the bound object (this must be an **OLE Object** type field).

▷ If necessary, modify the text for the control's label.

▷ Click ▨ ▾ to show the form in Form view, display the record in which you wish to insert the object, then click to select the object frame within the record.

▷ **Insert - Object**

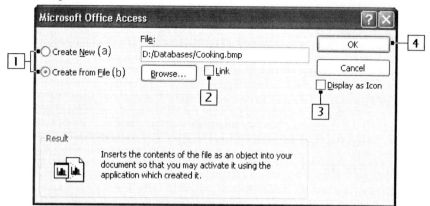

---

1 If you need to create the object in its application, activate option (a) then select the type of object you want to create.
If the object already exists, activate option (b) then use the **Browse** button to select it in your files.

2 If the **Create from File** option is active, you can tick this option if you want to create a link between the Access document and the object (rather than embedding it).

3 Activate this option if you wish to display a file icon, rather than the object itself.

4 Click to insert the object.

▷ If necessary, continue creating the object in its application, then close the server application window with **File - Exit** or click in the form.

▷ Save the changes made to the form then close it.

⇨ To delete the object, click in the object frame (in Form view) and press [Del].

⇨ The [🔼] tool is used to insert an unbound object: the object will be visible in all the pages of the form or report and it is not linked to a particular field in the table.

Modifying a bound object

▷ Display the form in Form view then double-click the object or its icon to start the server application.

If a link exists between the object and the document containing it, the object appears in a separate window.

▷ Make the required changes.

▷ For an embedded object, click anywhere in the client application window to retrieve the menus and tools of the client application.
For a linked object, close the server application window, saving the changes made.

⇨ *To modify an unbound object, proceed as if you were editing a bound object.*

Managing OLE links

▷ In Form view, click the frame of the OLE object concerned.

▷ **Edit - OLE/DDE Links**

opens the document corresponding to the selected link
closes the dialog box

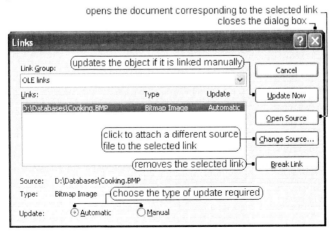

updates the object if it is linked manually

click to attach a different source file to the selected link

removes the selected link

choose the type of update required

DESIGN VIEW

6.2 Unbound controls

A- Creating a label

▷ Show the design of the form or report concerned.

▷ Click the ![Aa] tool button to select it on the toolbox (![icon]).

▷ Drag to draw the frame for the label.

You can also click and start typing: the label will get bigger as you enter its text.

▷ Type the label text: use the ⏷Shift Enter keys to go to a new line. Press Enter to confirm.

▷ Save the changes made to the form or report then close it.

⇒ *To edit the text in a label, select the label, point to the text in the label and click. Make your changes and confirm.*

⇒ *To adapt the size of a label to its contents, select the label concerned then use the* **Format - Size - To Fit** *command. You can also use this technique to make a frame fit the image it contains.*

⇒ *After you have used a tool, the ![cursor icon] tool button becomes active automatically. If you want a tool to remain active after you have used it, double-click its button to select it.*

B- Drawing a rectangle or line

▷ Show the form or report concerned in Design view.

▷ If it is hidden, display the toolbox (![icon]) then click the ![icon] tool button if you want to draw a rectangle or the ![icon] tool button to draw a line.

▷ Drag to draw the required shape.

▷ Save the changes made to the form or report then close it if necessary.

C- Creating a tab control

▷ Open the form concerned in Design view.

▷ Click the ![icon] tool button on the tool box (![icon]).

▷ Drag to draw the tab control in the form window.

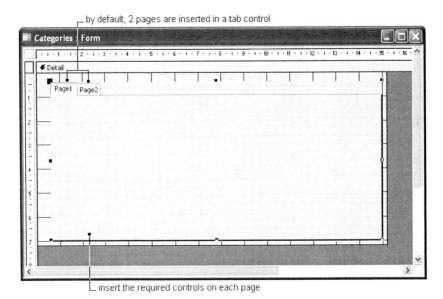

by default, 2 pages are inserted in a tab control

Categories : Form

Detail

Page1   Page2

insert the required controls on each page

▷ To go to a page, click its tab.

▷ To rename a page, click its tab, display the property sheet, then give the new name in the **Caption** property on the **Format** page.

▷ To insert a new page, right-click any tab, then choose **Insert Page**.

▷ To delete a page, right-click its tab, then click **Delete Page**.

▷ To arrange the pages in a different order, right-click any tab then choose **Page Order**.

▷ If you wish, click the [⊞ ▾] tool button to view the results.

▷ Save the changes made to the form then close it.

⇨ *Each page has specific properties, as does the tab control itself. To show a page's property sheet, click the tab then click the [⊞] tool button; to show the tab control's properties, click the blank space to the right of the tabs.*

D-Inserting a page break

Inserting a page break in a form or report ensures that a new page will start at that point on the printed copy.

▷ Show the form or report in Design view.

▷ Click the [⊟] tool button on the toolbox ([⚒]).

▷ In the window, click the place where Access should make a page break.

No matter where you click, the page break control (a small dashed line) always appears at the far left of the line.

▷ Save the changes made to the form or report then close the form or report if required.

⇨ *To delete a page break, select the control and press* [Del].

DESIGN VIEW

E- Inserting a picture

The picture will be visible on all the pages of the form or report; it is not linked to a table field or an external object.

▷ Show the form or report in Design view.

▷ Click the 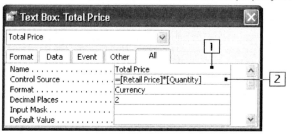 tool button on the toolbox, then drag to draw the outline for the picture.

▷ Select the drive then the folder in which the image file is stored then double-click the document's name.

The image can be in vector format (wmf, cgm, etc.) or bitmap format (bmp, pcx, tif, etc.).

▷ Save the changes made to the form or report then close it if necessary.

6.3 Calculated controls

A- Creating a calculated control

You can use this technique in a form or report to show a value that is calculated from one or more fields.

▷ Open the form or report in Design view, then select the ⌊abl⌋ tool button on the tool-box.

▷ Drag to draw the control's frame, then click the **All** tab on the property sheet.

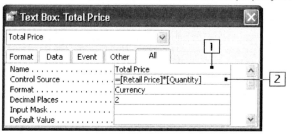

1 Give the control a name.

2 Type an equals sign (=) then enter the expression that Access will use to calculate the control value or click the ⌊...⌋ button to start the Expression Builder. This expression can include the name(s) of one or more fields in the source table (field names must be placed in square brackets), mathematical operators (such as *, +, -, /...), parentheses to indicate the order in which operations must be performed, the concatenation operator &, text (which should be entered between quotation marks), or various functions (mathematical, statistical, etc.).

Here are some examples:

This expression	Performs this action
[Price]*[Tax]	calculates the amount of tax.
[Title]&" "&[Surname]	concatenates the Title and Surname fields.
Month([Contact Date])	extracts the month from the value in the Contact Date field.
Sum([Quantity])	calculates the sum of the values in the Quantity field.

▷ Save the changes made to the form or report then if required, close it.

⇨ Use an expression of this type: **Function([field])** to insert a statistical function, such as Avg([Page number]) or Count([Client code]).

⇨ In a report with grouped records, the location of your expression determines on which records it performs its calculation.

⇨ The Now() function returns today's date, the Page() function can be used to number the pages of a form or report. You can also use the **Date and Time** and **Page Numbers** options in the **Insert** menu to insert the corresponding controls in the active section.

B - Setting conditions for a calculation

▷ Show the form or report in Design view then select the ▣ tool button on the toolbox.

▷ Drag to draw the control's frame then click the **All** tab on the control's property sheet.

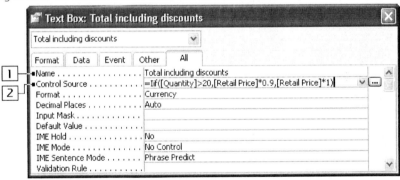

1 Give a name for the control.

2 Type an equals sign then enter the expression, using the Iif function and respecting the following syntax: **Iif (expression,result_if_true, result_if_false)**. The result of this function can be text (entered between quotation marks (")), a numerical value (unformatted), a date or another expression (such as [Quantity]*10).

▷ Save the changes made to the form or report then close it, if required.

⇨ You can test several conditions by linking the expressions by the operator AND or OR. For example:
IIf([Date]>#01/01/02#AND[Retail Price] >=1000,[Retail Price]*0.9,[Retail Price]).

C - Using the expression builder

The expression builder helps you to set out a calculation formula.

▷ Show the form or report in Design view, select the [abl] tool button in the toolbox then drag to draw the frame of the control.

▷ Click the **Control Source** property on the **Data** page then click the [...] button.

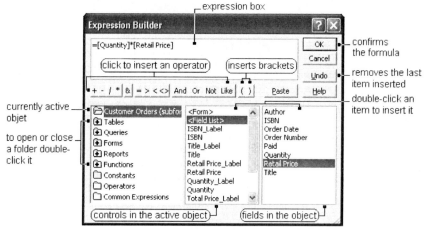

expression box

currently active objet

to open or close a folder double-click it

confirms the formula

removes the last item inserted

double-click an item to insert it

controls in the active object

fields in the object

⇨ *To insert text, type it into the expression box.*

6.4 Managing controls

A - Selecting controls

▷ Show the form or report in Design view then make sure the [⬚] tool button is active in the toolbox.

▷ To select a text box and its accompanying label, click the text box.

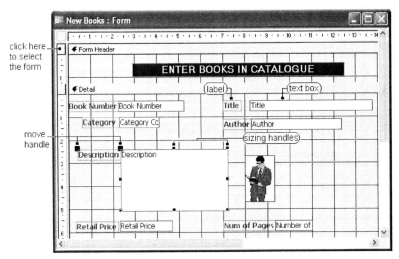

Handles appear around the selected elements. The name of the selected control appears in the first list box on the **Formatting** toolbar.

▷ To select a label without its text box, click just the label.

*In this case, **sizing handles** surround the label.*

▷ To select several controls, drag to draw a selection rectangle around them, or click the first control, hold down the ⌈⇧ Shift⌋ key then click the other controls to select them.

▷ To select all the controls situated along a vertical or horizontal axis, click the ruler at that axis then drag along the ruler to extend the selection area.

▷ To cancel the current selection, click anywhere else in the form or report.

⇨ *The **Select All** option in the **Edit** menu or ⌈Ctrl⌋ **A** can be used to select all the controls on the form or report. There is also an option you can use to **Select Form** or **Select Report**.*

⇨ *The **Selection behaviour** options, which can be found in **Tools - Options - Forms/Reports** tab, indicate whether you can partially enclose objects when making a multiple selection (this is the default option) or if you have to enclose them completely.*

B - Moving controls

▷ Display the form or report in Design view and make sure the [cursor] tool button is active in the toolbox, then select the control(s) concerned.

▷ To move a text box <u>and</u> its label, point to one of text box edges (the pointer takes the shape of a hand).
To move either the text box <u>or</u> the label, point to the control's move handle (the pointer takes the shape of a hand with a pointing finger).

▷ Drag the control to its new position; hold down the ⌈Ctrl⌋ key if you don't want the control to be snapped (attracted) to the points on the magnetic grid.

▷ Save the changes made to the form or report then close it.

DESIGN VIEW

Access 2003

⇨ If the **Snap to Grid** option is active in the **Format** menu, the controls will be attracted towards points on the window's magnetic grid when you move them.

⇨ You can force controls to move in a horizontal or vertical line by holding down the ⟨⇧ Shift⟩ key as you drag them (make sure you press the ⟨⇧ Shift⟩ key before the mouse button).

⇨ To copy or move controls from one section to another, use the **Copy** or **Cut** commands from the **Edit** menu.

C - Deleting controls

▷ Show the form or report concerned in Design view then make sure the ⬚ tool button is active.

▷ Select the controls concerned: to delete a text box along with its label, click the text box, or to delete just a label, without the text box attached to it, click in the label.

▷ Press the ⟨Del⟩ key.

▷ Save the changes made to the form or report then close it.

⇨ If you delete a text box, its associated label is deleted automatically.

D - Resizing a control

▷ Show the form or report concerned in Design view and make sure the ⬚ tool button is active.

▷ Select the control concerned, then point to one of the sizing handles.

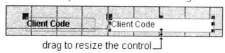

drag to resize the control

▷ Save the changes made to the form or report then close it.

⇨ You can set the width of a control in its property sheet.

⇨ Activate the **Can Grow** and **Can Shrink** options on the **Format** page of a control's property sheet so that the height of the control is adjusted to fit its contents when it is printed.

⇨ It is possible to adapt the size of a label to the length of the text, by the command **Format - Size - To Fit**.

⇨ The **Format - Size - To Grid** command is used to resize a selected control so it aligns with the nearest points on the grid.

⇨ To standardise the size of a selected set of controls, use the **Format - Size** command and take one of the last four options.

E - Aligning controls to each other

▷ Show the form or report in Design view and activate the ⬚ tool.

▷ Select the controls concerned then use **Format - Align**.

▷ Select one of the following options:

Left   aligns the left edges of all the controls with the one furthest to the left.

Right   aligns the right edges of the controls with the one furthest to the right.

Top   aligns the top edges of the controls with the one highest up.

Bottom   aligns the bottom edges of the controls with the one lowest down.

To Grid   snaps the top left corner of the controls to the closest point on the grid.

▷ Save the object and close it.

⇨ The **Top** and **Bottom** options are available only if the selected controls belong to the same section.

F- Standardising the space between controls

▷ Show the form or report concerned in Design view and make sure the ⬚ tool button is active, then select the controls concerned.

▷ **Format** - **Horizontal Spacing** or **Vertical Spacing**

▷ Choose one of the options proposed:

Make Equal   equalises space between the controls.

Increase   equalises space between the controls, and increases it by the size of one of the grid's rows/columns.

Decrease   equalises space between the controls, and decreases it by the size of one of the grid's rows/ columns.

▷ Save the changes made to the form or report then close it.

G- Displaying a control at the front/back

▷ Show the form or report concerned in Design view and make sure the ⬚ tool button is active in the toolbox, then select the control concerned.

▷ Use the **Format** - **Bring to Front** or **Send to Back** command.

▷ Save the changes made to the form or report then close it.

⇨ If a control is at the back, you can select it only if part of it is accessible; otherwise you first have to select the controls in front of it, and send them to the back!

H- Grouping/ungrouping controls

▷ Show the form or report concerned in Design view and make sure the ⬚ tool button is active.

▷ Select the controls you wish to group, or ungroup.

▷ Choose either **Group** or **Ungroup** in the **Format** menu.

The controls are enclosed within a rectangle (or group rectangle).

▷ To make modifications to the group (move it, resize it, change its presentation, etc.), select the group by selecting the group rectangle. To work on one control within a group, select the control concerned.

Click once on a group element to select the group. Once the group is selected, click a control within the group to select that control.

▷ Save the changes made to the form or report then close it.

⇨ *The **Ungroup** option is not available when two or more control groups are selected.*

I- Hiding a control on the screen/when printing

▷ Show the form in Design view and activate 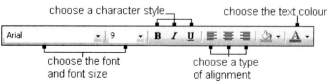 if necessary.

▷ Open the **Format** page of the property sheet and set the value of the **Display When** property:

Always   the control is visible on the screen and in print.

Print Only   the control appears in the printed form/report but not on the screen.

Screen Only   the control is visible on the screen, but it is not printed.

▷ Save the changes and close the form.

J- Modifying the presentation of text in a control

▷ Open the form or report in Design view then make sure the tool button is active.

▷ Select the controls containing the text then use the appropriate buttons on the **Formatting** toolbar:

▷ Save the changes made to the object then close it.

⇨ *All of these properties can also be found on the control's property sheet.*

K- Modifying the presentation of controls/sections

▷ Open the form or report in Design view then make sure the tool button is active.

▷ Select the controls concerned or click the section title to select it.

▷ Use the last buttons on the **Formatting** toolbar:

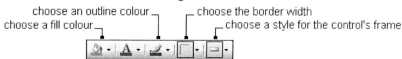

▷ Save the changes made to the object then close it.

⇨ *Many of the buttons on the **Formatting** toolbar change constantly, always representing the last option selected. To reapply the last option used, you need only click the button, without opening the attached list.*

L- Copying one control's presentation onto another

▷ Show the form or report concerned in Design view and make sure the ![tool] tool button is active.

▷ Select the control whose presentation you want to copy.

▷ Click the ![tool] tool button, then click the control to which you wish to apply the copied format.

▷ Save the changes made to the form or report then close it.

⇨ *If you activate the* ![tool] *tool with a double-click, it will stay active, allowing you to copy the presentation onto several target controls. Press* Esc *to stop the format painting process.*

M -Changing the format of the values in a control

▷ Show the form or report concerned in Design view and make sure the ![tool] tool button is active.

▷ Select the control concerned, display its property sheet, then click the **Format** tab.

▷ In the **Format** property, select the required format.

▷ If required, give the number of decimal places to use, in the **Decimal Places** property.

▷ Save the changes made to the form or report and close it.

⇨ *All of these properties can also be found on the control's property sheet.*

⇨ *You can devise your own custom formats in the* **Format** *property of the control concerned.*

⇨ *To convert a monetary value to euros and vice versa, use the* **EuroConvert** *function.*

N-Modifying the presentation of pages in a tab control

▷ Show the form concerned in Design view and make sure the ![tool] tool button is active.

▷ To modify the presentation of pages in a tab control, start by double- clicking one of the page tabs to show its property sheet. Click the **Format** tab then define the page presentation using these properties: **Caption, Picture, Picture Type, Page Index** and **Visible**.

▷ To modify the presentation of the tab control, double-click one of its edges or the empty space to the right of the tabs. Click the **Format** tab then define the control's presentation using these properties: **Visible, Back Style, Multi Row, Style, Tab Fixed Height** and **Tab Fixed Width**

You can use the last properties in the list to change the presentation of the text on the page tabs.

▷ Save the changes made to the form then close it.

O -Modifying the default format for controls

▷ Show the form or report in Design view.

▷ Select a control with the parameters that you want to activate by default.

▷ **Format - Set Control Defaults**

If you create a new control of the same type, it will have the same characteristics as the one you selected.

▷ Save the form or report then close it.

P- Creating conditional formats

▷ Show the form or report concerned in Design view and make sure the ⬚ tool button is active.

▷ Select the control concerned, then use **Format - Conditional Formatting**.

▷ In the **Condition 1** frame, choose the **Field Value Is** option if the condition refers to the selected control values or the **Expression Is** option, if the condition refers to an expression.

*The **Field Has Focus** option lets you modify the format of the selected control.*

▷ If the condition refers to field values, choose a comparison operator then enter a value in the text box.

If the condition refers to an expression, type the expression in the text box.

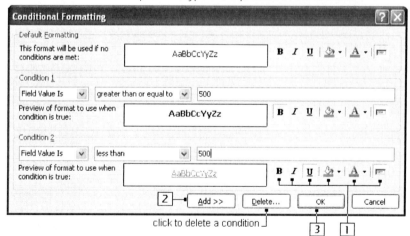

click to delete a condition ⌐

1 Use the available tools to define the format which will be applied if the condition is met.

2 To define other formats for other conditions (especially which format to apply if the previous condition is not met), click this button. You can define three conditions in this way.

3 Click to confirm the formats.

▷ Save the changes made to the form or report then close it.

Q-Adding a Smart Tag to a control or field

Smart Tags help you carry out some common actions more quickly, such as sending a message or opening a contact's details.

▷ Open the query, form or data access page in Design view ⟨Design⟩.

▷ Select the control or field in which you want to add a Smart Tag, activate the **Data** tab (or **General** for a query) on its property sheet, click the **SmartTags** property and click its ⟨...⟩ button.

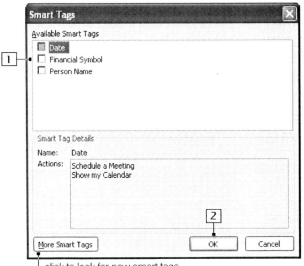

└ click to look for new smart tags

1 Tick the check box(es) of the smart tags you want to attach to the chosen field or control.

2 Click the **OK** button to confirm.

▷ Display the form in Form view ⟨▦ ▾⟩, the query in Datasheet view ⟨▦ ▾⟩ or the data access page in Page view ⟨▦ ▾⟩ to check that smart tags have been correctly added to the control(s) or field(s) in question.

▷ To use a smart tag, show the record concerned then point to the value of the control or the field that contains the smart tag, so you can see the ⟨ⓘ⟩ button. Click the ⟨ⓘ⟩ button to open its list, which contains the Smart Tag actions associated with the active field or control.

Access 2003

Click the option for the action you want to carry out.

▷ Save the changes you have made to the query, form or data access page then, if you have finished with it, close the object.

⇒ A Smart Tag can also be added to a table field (in Design view) using the **Smart Tags** field property.

⇒ To remove one of the Smart Tags attached to a control or field, display the **Smart Tags** dialog box for that field or control (click the [...] button on the **Smart Tags** property of the field or control in question) then deactivate the check box for each Smart Tag you want to remove.

⇒ To remove all the Smart Tags attached to a control or field, delete the contents of the **Smart Tags** property in the property sheet of the field or control in question.

6.5 Sections

A - Showing/hiding sections

▷ Show the form or report concerned in Design view and make sure the 🔲 tool button is active.

▷ Open the **View** menu to activate or deactivate the **Page Header/Footer** and/or **Form** (or **Report**) **Header/Footer** options.

▷ If you try to hide sections that contain controls, Access displays a message to inform you that all the controls will be deleted. Click **Yes** to hide the sections and delete the controls or **No** to cancel hiding the sections.

▷ Save the changes made to the form or report and close it.

B- Changing the height of a section

▷ Show the form or report concerned in Design view and make sure the ⬚ tool button is active.

▷ Point to the top of the next section's title bar.

▷ Drag upwards or downwards, to decrease or increase the height of the section.

▷ Save the changes made to the form or report and close it.

⇨ *Data in the **Page Header** and **Page Footer** sections appear at the top and bottom of each page in the form or report.*

⇨ *Data in the **Form** (or **Report**) **Header** and **Form** (or **Report**) **Footer** sections appear on the first page of the form (or report) or on the last page.*

7.1 Select queries

Select queries allow you to select records according to one or more criteria.

A-Creating a single table query

Without a wizard

▷ Click **Queries** in the objects bar then click the **New** button on the database window, or click **Queries** in the objects bar then click the **Create query in Design view** shortcut, or open the list on the **New Object** (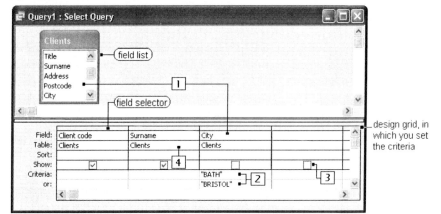) tool button then click the **Query** option (you can also use the **Insert - Query** command).

▷ Select the **Design View** option and click **OK**.

The ***New Query*** *dialog box does not appear when you use the* ***Create query in Design view*** *shortcut.*

▷ Select the name of the object you wish to add to the query, click the **Add** button then click **Close**.

design grid, in which you set the criteria

1. Drag the fields from the field list onto the design grid: these will appear in the datasheet containing the query results. Double-clicking a field also inserts it into the design grid.

2. Enter the selection criteria (cf. 7.1 - E - Setting query criteria).

3. If you set criteria on a field but do not want that field to appear in the results, deactivate the **Show** check box.

4. Give a sort order, if appropriate: if you wish to sort by several fields, put the first field that you wish to sort by on the left of the grid, followed by the second field to be sorted, and so on.

▷ To see the query's result, go into Datasheet view by clicking the [tool button] tool button or run the query with the [tool button] tool button.

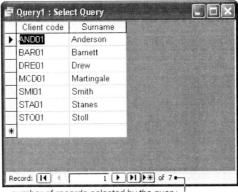

number of records selected by the query

This datasheet can be used like any other datasheet based on a table. You can modify the data it contains and these changes will be carried over automatically into the source table.

Click *if you want to return to the query's Design view.*

▷ To save the query, use the **File - Save** command or 🖫 or Ctrl **S**, give it a name and click **OK**.

▷ If necessary, close the query.

⇨ *You can interrupt a query that is running by pressing* Ctrl Break *.*

⇨ *To change the title of a column in the result datasheet, enter the name of the field on which it is based in the design grid using this syntax:* **column name:field name***.*

⇨ *The design grid used to create a query is identical to the grid used to create advanced filters.*

⇨ *To define a query's properties, show its property sheet by double-clicking the grey area at the top of the design grid window then use the* **Output All Fields***,* **Top Values***,* **Unique Values***,* **Unique Records** *and* **Run Permissions** *properties.*

With a wizard

▷ Click **Queries** in the objects bar then click the **New** button on the database window, or click **Queries** in the objects bar then click the **Create query by using wizard** shortcut,

or open the drop-down list on the **New Object** tool button (🖅 ▼) and click the **Query** option (or use **Insert - Query**).

▷ Select the **Simple Query Wizard** option and click **OK**.

The **New Query** *dialog box does not appear if you use the* **Create query by using wizard** *shortcut.*

▷ In the **Tables/Queries** list box, select the table or query on which your new query will be based.

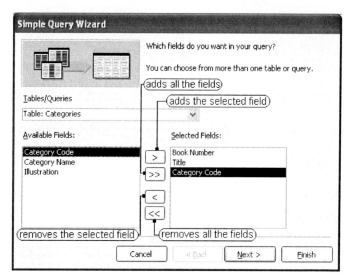

▷ Insert the fields you want to use in the query (cf. illustration above) and click **Next**.

▷ If you want the query to group certain records to make statistical calculations, activate the **Summary** option.

▷ Click **Next**, then enter the title that should appear on the query's title bar (this title is also the name under which the query will be saved).

▷ Choose one of the options depending on whether you wish to go straight to the result datasheet or to the query's structure in Design view, then click the **Finish** button.

▷ To show the query in Design view so that you can modify its structure, click the tool button.

▷ Proceed as you would if you were creating the query without a wizard.

▷ Save the changes made to the query then close it.

B- Creating a multiple table query with a wizard

▷ If you have not already done it, establish the relationships between the tables you want to use in your multiple table query.

▷ Click **Queries** in the objects bar then click the ⬛New button.

▷ Select the **Simple Query Wizard** option then click **OK**.

▷ In the **Tables/Queries** list, select the first table or query from which you want to create the new query, then insert the fields you want to use in the query.

▷ In the **Tables/Queries** list, select the second table or query you want to insert into the query. In the same way, insert the fields from this second table or query into the **Selected Fields** list, making sure the same fields do not appear twice.

▷ Proceed in the same way to insert any fields from other tables or queries, then click **Next**.

▷ If you want the query to group certain records to make statistical calculations, activate the **Summary** option. Otherwise, leave the **Detail** option active. Click **Next**.

▷ Enter the title that should appear on the query's title bar, then choose one of the options depending on whether you wish to go straight to the results datasheet (first option) or to the query's structure (second option).

▷ Click the **Finish** button.

▷ To show the query in Design view, to work in the query grid, click [icon].

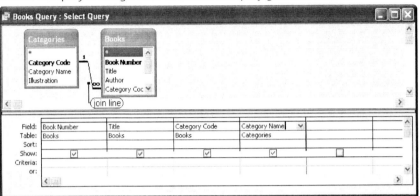

Even if the tables or queries are not related, Access will create a join automatically, should it find a common field between in the two tables/queries.

▷ Work with the query design grid as you would for a single table query.

▷ Click the [icon] tool button to view the results.

*By default, Access creates an **inner-join** relationship between the tables in the query. Only records with counterparts in the other table appear in the datasheet.*

▷ Save the changes made to the query then close it.

⇨ *To add or remove tables in a query, proceed as though you were working in the **Relationships** window (cf. 3.2 - Table relationships - B - Managing relationships in a database.*

⇨ *If you double-click the join line linking two tables, you can change the join type in a multiple table query.*

⇨ *To create a multiple table query without using a wizard, proceed as though you were making a single table query, but add several tables or queries into the grid from the **Show Table** dialog box.*

C - Managing the query grid

▷ Select the query concerned and click [icon].

▷ To remove one or more fields from the query design grid, select them and press [Del]. To remove all the fields from the grid, use the **Edit - Clear Grid** command.

▷ To add all the fields in a table into the design grid, double-click the table's title bar then drag the selection onto the first empty cell in the **Field** row in the design grid. You can also drag the * symbol from the first row of the field list onto the design grid.

▷ To move a field, point to the field selector then click to select it. Drag the field selector: a thick vertical line appears. Place this line in the position where you wish to put the field.

▷ To insert a field into the design grid, select it in the table then drag it towards the design grid. Choose the field in front of which you wish to place it and drag it onto that field.

▷ The **Insert - Rows** command inserts a new row of criteria above the active row. The **Insert - Columns** command inserts a new column to the left of the active column.

▷ Save the changes made then close the query.

⇒ The **Table Names** appear in the query grid if the option of the same name is active in the **View** menu.

D-Running a query

▷ There are two ways of running a query:

- if you are in the database window, double-click the icon of the query you want to run.

- click **Queries** in the objects bar, select the name of the query you want to run, click the ⟨⟨ Design⟩ button then the ⟨ ! ⟩ tool button.

▷ If you wish, close the query datasheet window when you have finished.

E- Setting query criteria

▷ Show the query in Design view.

▷ On the **Criteria** row, click the column of the required field and enter your criterion according to the following principles:

Field type	How to set criteria	Examples
Number, Currency or AutoNumber	enter just the value, without any formatting.	1500.45
Date/Time	enter the date or time in the format of your choice; the data may be typed between # signs.	01/01/05 >#01/01/05# 01 January 2005 01-Jan-2005
Yes/No	enter values corresponding to Yes enter values corresponding to No	Yes, True, On or -1 No, False, Off or 0

▷ Set the criterion using the comparison operators (there are six of them): < (Less than), <= (Less than or equals), > (Greater than), >= (Greater than or equals), = (Equals), <> (Different from).

▷ Other operators can also be used in Access:

Operator	Selects records	Examples
Between	with field value that fall between two given values.	Between "A" and "C" Between 10 and 20 Between 01/01/05 and 02/02/05
In	with field values that are included in a given list.	In ("BERLIN", "LONDON")
Is	with a blank or nonblank field.	Is Null Is Not Null
Like	with data that meets an approximate criterion.	Like "*ave*"
Not	with data that does not meet the criterion.	Is Not Null Not In ("BERLIN", "LONDON")

▷ If you want to set several criteria, to be checked simultaneously, insert them <u>all in the same row</u> in the columns representing the corresponding fields (if the criteria refer to the same field, separate them with the AND operator).
If one or other of the criteria has to be met, insert them in different rows.

▷ Click the [🔽] tool button to view the result.

▷ Save the changes made to the query then close it.

⇨ *Criteria expressions can also contain functions (in this case, field names must be placed in square brackets). For example:*
Year([Date of birth])=1966 selects all the recorded people born in 1966.
Month([Date of birth])=10 selects the clients born in October.
<Date()-30 selects the clients contacted 30 days ago (the Date() function calculates the current date).

⇨ *If you are entering a very long criterion, you can press* [⇧ Shift] [F2] *to display the* **Zoom** *window.*

F - Creating a parameter query

When you run a query, Access selects records from the source table according to the criteria defined in the query. It is also possible to set these criteria not actually in the query, but when you are running it: for this, you create a **parameter query**.

▷ Show the query in Design view, then enter the items in the query grid as usual.

▷ Instead of defining selection criteria, type the prompt text between square brackets in the column(s) representing the field(s) concerned by the selection criteria. This prompt will appear when you run the query.

Field:	Title	First Name	Last Name	City	
Table:	Clients	Clients	Clients	Clients	
Sort:					
Show:	☑	☑	☑	☑	
Criteria:				[Specify required city:]	
or:					

Make sure the prompt is not identical to the field name.

▷ Click 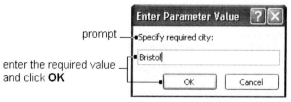 to run the query.

```
Enter Parameter Value  [?][X]

prompt ──── •Specify required city:

enter the required value ── •|Bristol|
and click OK
                          [    OK    ]  [   Cancel   ]
```

▷ Save the query and, if you wish, close it.

G-Creating a crosstab query

Access provides an effective tool for summarising data from several tables: the **crosstab query**.

City	Total Of Total	Chris TANNER	Neil McDERMOTT	Pauline FREARS
▶ Abbeyville	165	149	16	
Beecham	60		6	54
Cleveden	721	30	101	590
Eastport	64	41	11	12
Emerald Bay	124	96	28	
Herston	16		16	
Keaton Hill	114	37	63	14
Killybill	150	66	84	
Lancaster	309		98	211
Lorton	714	405	300	9
Moreton	55		41	14
Mt Rush	172	68	90	14
Oak Grove	222			222
Rafter	162		155	7
St Lucia	102	30		72
Stoughton	136	27	89	20
Tewesbury	844	223	392	229

Record: [I◀] ◀ [1 ▶][▶I]▶* of 17

▷ Create a new query (without using a wizard), including the tables and queries needed for the crosstab query spreadsheet.

▷ Transform the query into a crosstab query using the **Query** - **Crosstab** command, or by opening the list on the **Query Type** tool button and choosing **Crosstab**.

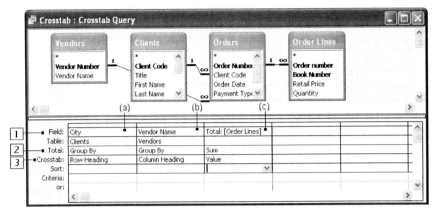

1. Insert the three following fields into the query design grid:

   (a) the field whose values will be used as row headings in the crosstab query spreadsheet,

   (b) the field whose values will be used as column headings in the crosstab query spreadsheet,

   (c) the field containing the values forming the basis of the crosstab query spreadsheet.

2. Enter the operation which will calculate the table values in the appropriate column. For the other columns, the value in the **Total** row should be **Group By**.

3. Indicate for each field whether the values it contains should appear as a **Row Heading**, a **Column Heading**, or as a **Value** in the datasheet.

▷ Click the ⬚ tool button to run the query.

▷ Save the query and close it.

⇨ *You can insert several row headings, but only one column heading.*

⇨ *A crosstab query can be used as the basis of a chart.*

⇨ *The Crosstab Query Wizard can be used if all the data needed in the spreadsheet is contained in one table or query.*

H-Creating a find-unmatched query

Access can use a find-unmatched query to pick out records from one table which have no matching records in a related table.

▷ Click **Queries** on the objects bar and click the ⬚New button.

▷ Choose the **Find Unmatched Query Wizard** then click **OK**.

▷ In the list, select the table that contains the records you want to show with the find-unmatched query and click **Next** to move on.

▷ Next, select the table or query that contains the related records you want to compare with the previously selected object. Click **Next** once you have done that.

The field which is common to both tables is generally selected in each list: remember that the common field may not have exactly the same name in each table.

▷ If the related field has not been selected automatically, select the appropriate field in both tables (or queries) and click the <=> button.

▷ Click **Next** to move on to the next step and indicate which fields to include in the query datasheet, as you would if you were using the Simple Query Wizard.

▷ Click **Next** to move on to the next step and give a name under which to save the new query; this is the name which will appear on its title bar.

▷ Either leave the first option active to run the query and see the records it selects or choose the second option to go into its Design view. Then, click the **Finish** button.

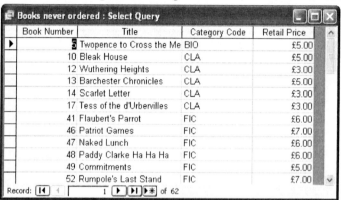

This query selects books that have not yet been ordered.

▷ If you want to change the query's design in some way, click the  tool button.

▷ Save the changes made to the query and close it if required.

I - Creating a find-duplicates query

Access can use a find-duplicates query to locate records in the same table or query with identical field values.

▷ Click **Queries** on the objects bar then click the New button.

▷ Choose the **Find Duplicates Query Wizard** option then click **OK**.

▷ In the list, select the table that contains the records you want to show with the find-duplicates query and click **Next** to move on.

▷ Select the fields from the source object that may contain duplicate values, as you would if you were using the Simple Query Wizard. Click **Next** to move on to the next step.

▷ In addition to the fields that may contain duplicates, add any other fields that you want the query to display and click **Next**.

▷ Give a name under which to save the new query; this is the name which will appear on its title bar.

▷ Either leave the first option active to run the query and see the records it selects or choose the second option to go into its Design view. Then, click the **Finish** button.

	Title	Category Code	Book Number	Author
▶	Persuasion	CLA	125	Austen, Jane
	Persuasion	CLA	15	Austen, Jane
	Simisola	CRI	126	Rendell, Ruth
	Simisola	CRI	26	Rendell, Ruth
	Year in Provence	TRA	127	Mayle, Peter
	Year in Provence	TRA	111	Mayle, Peter
*			(AutoNumber)	

Duplicate Book Titles : Select Query

Record: 1 of 6

*This query selects book records that have identical values in the **Title** and **Author** fields.*

▷ If you want to change the query's design in some way, click the tool button.

▷ Save the changes made to the query and close it if required.

7.2 Calculations in queries

A- Inserting a calculated field in a query

▷ With the query in Design view, click an empty space on the **Field** row.

▷ Give the name of the calculated field followed by the corresponding expression. Use the **Name:expression** format.

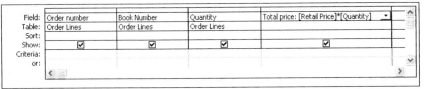

Field:	Order number	Book Number	Quantity	Total price: [Retail Price]*[Quantity] ▾
Table:	Order Lines	Order Lines	Order Lines	
Sort:				
Show:	☑	☑	☑	☑
Criteria:				
or:				

▷ Click the tool button to run the query and view the results.

▷ Save the changes made to the query then close it.

B- Calculating statistics without grouping

You can perform a statistical calculation on all the records in a table or on a group of records, selected with a set of criteria. For example, you can calculate the number of clients in a table, or the number of clients living in a certain town.

▷ Show the query in Design view. In the query design grid, insert the field on which you wish to make your calculation.

▷ Click the Σ tool button to display the **Total** row.

Field:	Client Code	Title
Table:	Clients	Clients
Total:	Count	Where
Sort:		
Show:	☑	☐
Criteria:		"Mrs"
or:		"Ms"

| 1 | 3 | 2 |

1 Choose the type of statistical calculation you wish to use.

2 If they are not all to be inserted, insert the fields on which the selection criteria are based and choose the **Where** operation for these fields (the **Show** option is deactivated automatically).

3 Set the criteria in the usual way.

▷ Click the tool button to run the query.

▷ Save the changes made to the query then close it.

⇨ *You will see the result of the statistical calculation but not the record details.*

C - Calculating statistics on groups

▷ Show the query in Design view.

▷ Click the Σ tool button to display the **Total** row.

There are three ways in which you might want to calculate statistics on a group of records.

▷ You might perform one statistical calculation per group of records, without applying selection criteria; for example, how many customers live in each town?

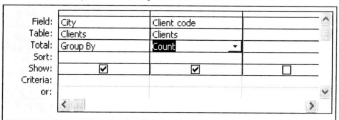

Field:	City	Client code	
Table:	Clients	Clients	
Total:	Group By	Count ▼	
Sort:			
Show:	☑	☑	☐
Criteria:			
or:			

▷ You might perform a statistical calculation on all the records in the table, then select groups of records meeting certain criteria; for example, you count the number of customers in each town then select the towns with more than 20 customers.

Field:	City	Client code	
Table:	Clients	Clients	
Total:	Group By	Count	
Sort:			
Show:	☑	☑	
Criteria:		>20	
or:			

▷ You might select certain records then make a statistical calculation on those records only; for example, you select the customers born after January 1970 then count how many there are in each town.

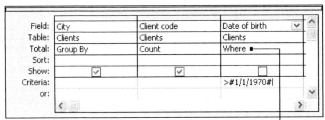

Field:	City	Client code	Date of birth	☑
Table:	Clients	Clients	Clients	
Total:	Group By	Count	Where ▪	
Sort:				
Show:	☑	☑	☐	
Criteria:			>#1/1/1970#|	
or:				

use the Where operator on the fields on which ⌐
the selection criteria are based

▷ Click the [image] tool button to run the query.

▷ Save the query then close it.

7.3 Action queries

A- Using a query to delete records

Delete queries can be used to extract and delete the records that meet your set criteria.

▷ Start by creating a select query that will extract the records you require.

▷ Click the [image] tool button to check the list of extracted records, then return to the query in Design view.

▷ To transform a select query into a delete query, use the **Query - Delete Query** command or open the drop-down list on the [image] tool button to select the **Delete Query** option.

Access 2003 91

▷ If you wish, save the query.

▷ Run the delete query: if you are in the database window, double-click the name of the query. If you are in Design view, click the [!] tool button.

▷ Click the **Yes** button to confirm the deletions.

B- Using a query to create a table

With this technique, you can create a new table from records in an existing table.

▷ Create a select query that will extract the records you wish to include in your new table. You should insert in this query all the fields that you want the new table to have.

▷ Click the [!] tool button to check the list of records then return to the query in Design view.

▷ Transform the select query into an action query using the **Query - Make Table Query** command or open the list on the [⊡ ▾] tool button and choose the **Make Table Query** option.

[1] Enter the name for the new table.

[2] Activate one of the options shown to indicate whether the table is to be created in the current database or in another database (in this case, give the database's **File Name** or **Browse** to select it).

[3] Click to create the table.

▷ Save the query if required then close it.

▷ To run the make-table query, double-click its name in the database window.

▷ Click **Yes** twice to confirm making the new table.

C- Updating certain records with a query

Update queries *are used to modify the values in selected fields.*

▷ Start by creating a select query that will extract the records you require: insert into this query only the field whose value must change and any fields on which you need to set criteria.

▷ Click the [!] tool button to check the list of extracted records, then return to the query in Design view.

▷ To transform a select query into an update query, use the **Query - Update Query** command or open the drop-down list on the 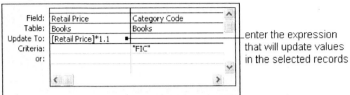 tool button and choose the **Update Query** option.

enter the expression
that will update values
in the selected records

▷ Click the ⚡ tool button to update the records, then click **OK** to confirm the update.

▷ Save the changes made to the query then close it.

8.1 Pivot tables

A- Creating a pivot table

A pivot table provides a structure for summarising and analysing data from one or more tables or queries.

Using the Pivot Table Wizard

▷ Click **Forms** in the objects bar then click the [⬚ New] button.

▷ Click the **PivotTable Wizard** option, open the drop-down list and select the table or query for which you want to create a pivot table form (you do this as if you were using the normal Form Wizard).

▷ Click **OK** then click **Next**.

▷ Specify which fields you wish to insert into the pivot table form (you do this as if you were using the normal Form Wizard).

▷ In the **Tables/Queries** list, if necessary, select the second table or query that you want to use for the pivot table form and insert the fields from this second table/query.

▷ If you need to insert fields from any other table or query, follow the same procedure, then click the **Finish** button.

*A form appears in **PivotTable View**.*

You can see a window containing the list of fields, but for now no field has been inserted into the pivot table.

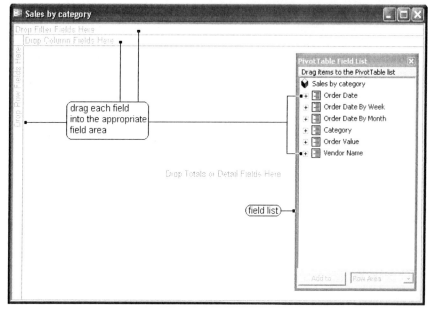

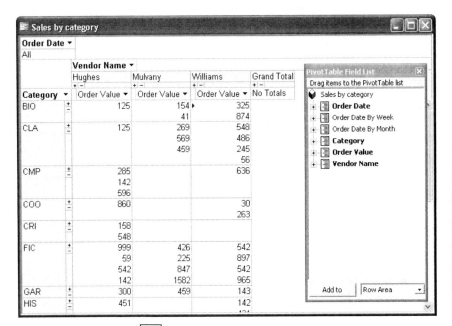

▷ Save the pivot table form (💾) and close it.

*Placing a field or fields in the **filter** area allows you to summarise all or certain elements of the field or to display the field's contents one by one.*

Without a wizard

▷ Double-click the name of the form, table or query you wish to use to create a pivot table form.

▷ Open the list on the 🔽 tool button and choose the **PivotTable View** option.

*The form, table or query appears in **PivotTable** view.*

▷ Define the table's layout by dragging each field from the **PivotTable Field List** window onto the required area in the pivot table (cf. previous subheading).

▷ Save the changes made to the form (💾) and close it.

B- Selecting an element in a pivot table form

▷ Double-click the name of the form concerned, and if necessary, display the form in PivotTable view.

▷ To select a single cell of data, click it.

▷ To select several adjacent cells of data, drag over the required cells until they all appear selected.

▷ To select a row, column, detail or total field, click the corresponding field label.

▷ To select an item in a row or column field, click the corresponding label.

Access 2003

▷ To select several non-adjacent items in a row or column field, click the first item then hold down the ⌈Ctrl⌋ key and click to select the others; to select adjacent items, click the first item then hold down the ⌈0 Shift⌋ key and click to select the last item.

Selecting an item selects all the data within it.

C- Changing what the pivot table displays

▷ Double-click the name of the object concerned, and if necessary, display the form in PivotTable view.

▷ To hide the details of a field item, click the ⊟ sign accompanying it and to display it, click the ⊞ sign.

▷ To hide the details of all the items in a pivot table, click one of its fields then use the **PivotTable - Hide Details** command or ▧. To display the details again, use the **PivotTable - Show Details** command or ▧.

You must hide all the details of all the pivot table items before adding a total to the table, otherwise no value will be visible in the detail area.

▷ To show or hide the items from a row, column, filter or detail field, click the down arrow next to the field name. Tick each item you want to show and deactivate all those you want to hide then confirm with **OK**.

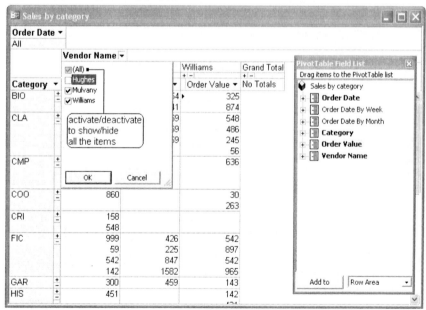

▷ Save the changes made to the object and close it.

D-Managing pivot table fields

▷ Double-click the name of the object concerned and make sure it is in Pivot Table view.

▷ To add a field to the pivot table, drag it from the **Pivot Table Field List** window (click the ▦ button if you cannot see this window) onto the appropriate area in the pivot table (row, column, filter or data area).

▷ To remove a pivot table field, drag the field clear of the pivot table, releasing the mouse button when a red cross appears next to the pointer: ✕.

The field disappears from the pivot table but not from the source data.

▷ To move a field in a pivot table, point to the corresponding field label until the pointer takes this shape: ✛. Drag the label to the required place in the pivot table.

▷ To move a row, column or filter area to a higher or lower level (only in the case where a row, column or filter area contains several fields), point to the corresponding field label then drag to the left (to move up a level) or to the right (to move down a level).

▷ To move a field item, click the item concerned, to select the whole row or column, then drag the selected item to its new position.

▷ To modify the name of a field, click the field concerned then click ▦ to show its property sheet. Click the **Captions** tab, and in the **Caption** text box, enter the new field name. Close the property sheet by clicking its ✕ button.

▷ Save the changes made to the form and close it.

⇨ *You can add several row, column and filter fields but only one detail field can be added.*

⇨ *By default, a data field (**Data Area**) summarises numerical data with the **Sum** function and non-numerical data with the **Count** function.*

⇨ *To format a field or field items, use the options under the **Format** and/or **Captions** tab in the **Properties** window ▦ of the field or items concerned.*

E- Grouping records in a pivot table

Grouping items by a given interval

*With this feature, you could, for example, group the items in an **Order Date** field by month.*

▷ Double-click the name of the object concerned, then, if necessary, display the form in PivotTable view.

▷ Click the field (row, column or filter) whose records you wish to group, show its property sheet ▦, and click the **Filter and Group** tab.

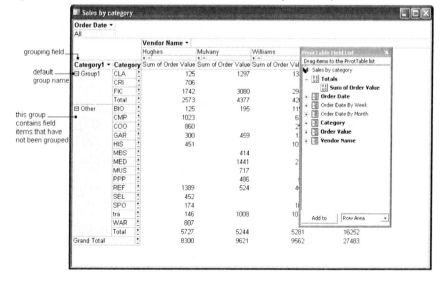

▷ Close the property sheet window, save the changes made to the object then close it.

⇨ To cancel a grouping, click the name of the field concerned, show its property sheet, click the **Filter and Group** tab and choose the (**No grouping**) option in the **Group items by** list.

Creating a custom group

▷ Double-click the name of the object concerned, and make sure it is in Pivot Table view.

▷ Select the field items (in a row or column) that you wish to group. Use ⇧ Shift -clicks to select adjacent items or Ctrl -clicks to select non-adjacent items.

▷ Right-click one of the selected items then click the **Group Items** option.

▷ If required, rename the custom group field and the custom group. To do this, select the name of the field or group, show its property sheet, click the **Captions** tab then enter the new name in the **Caption** text box.

▷ To expand or collapse the contents of a custom group, select the custom group concerned then click the ⊞ or ⊟ tool button.

▷ To expand or collapse all the groups in a custom group field, click the custom group field name then click the ⊞ or ⊟ tool button.

▷ Save the changes made to the object then close it.

⇒ To remove a custom group, right-click the name of the custom group and choose the **Clear Custom Grouping** option.

⇒ The options in the **Filtering** frame of the **Properties** window (**Filter and Group** tab) can be used to filter the records of the selected field.

⇒ You can also filter the records of a pivot table by using the ⊞ tool button on the **PivotTable** toolbar.

F- Adding a total field to a pivot table

You can add a total field only to the detail area.

▷ Double-click the name of the object concerned, then, if necessary, display the form in PivotTable view.

▷ Click the name of the field for which you wish to obtain statistics. If the field name is not visible, click the ▦ tool button to show all the details in the entire pivot table.

You can also click one of the values in the detail area.

▷ Click the Σ▾ tool button on the **PivotTable** toolbar then click the required statistical function (**Sum**, **Count**, **Min**, **Max**, etc.).

▷ Click one of the fields in the pivot table then, depending on your requirements, use the ⊞ or ⊟ tool button to show or hide the details of all the pivot table items.

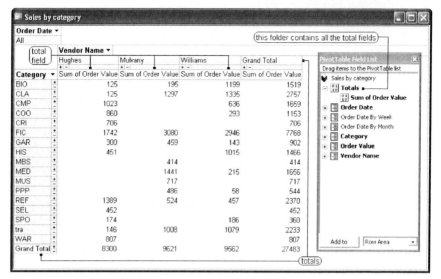

▷ Save the changes made to the object then close it.

⇨ *To remove a total field from the data source, show the field list if it is not visible* (📋) *then right-click the total field concerned and choose the* **Delete** *option. If you wish to remove the total field from the pivot table, proceed as for any other type of field (cf. Adding/removing pivot table fields in this chapter).*

G-Creating a calculated total field in a pivot table

You can create a calculated total field which calculates data in the pivot table by using an expression.

▷ Double-click the name of the form concerned, then if necessary, display the form in PivotTable view.

▷ **PivotTable**
Calculated Totals and Fields

▷ Click the **Create Calculated Total** option to create a total field or the **Create Calculated Detail Field** option to create a detail field.

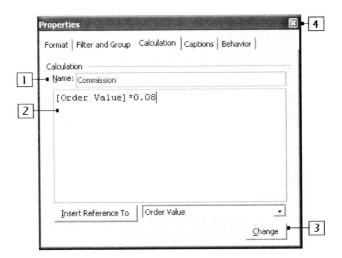

1 Enter the field name.

2 Click here and enter the required expression. To insert a field into your expression, select it in the list that you can see at the bottom of the **Properties** dialog box then click the **Insert Reference To** button.

3 Click this button.

4 Close the **Properties** dialog box.

▷ If you created a detail field, click the [icon] button to show all the details of all the items in the pivot table so you can see the new detail field.

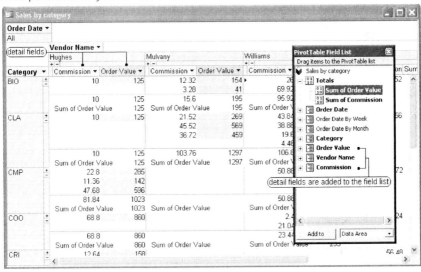

When you create a detail field, Access adds this to the **PivotTable Field List** while a total field is added to the **Totals** section in the same list.

▷ Save the changes made to the object and close it.

⇨ To modify the name and/or expression of a calculated field, select the field label, show its property sheet by clicking the 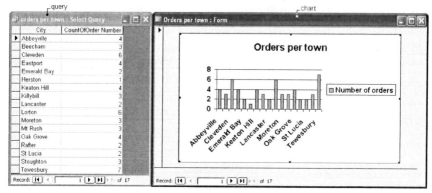 tool button then click the **Calculation** tab. Modify the field **Name** and/or its expression then click the **Change** button.

⇨ To show totals as percentages, select the total field concerned and choose one of the options under the **PivotTable** - **Show As** menu or %.

8.2 Charts

A- Creating a chart representing data in a table

*This is a technique for creating an **unbound** chart representing the values displayed in a table or query.*

▷ If necessary, create a query to bring together the data you want to see in the chart. The chart's source table should contain the fields with the numerical values to be represented, and the fields containing the labels identifying each value (in a bar, column or line type chart, these labels can be seen on the value axis).

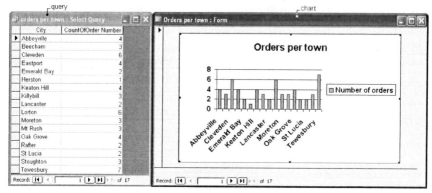

▷ In Design view, open the form or the report in which you want to create the graph.

▷ **Insert** - **Chart**

▷ In one of the sections, draw a frame for the chart.

▷ In the **View** frame, specify whether your data is contained in a table or query then select the table or query concerned then click **Next**.

▷ Select the fields containing the items needed for the chart (one or more fields must contain the values and another should contain their labels), then click **Next**.

▷ Click the required type of chart then click **Next**.

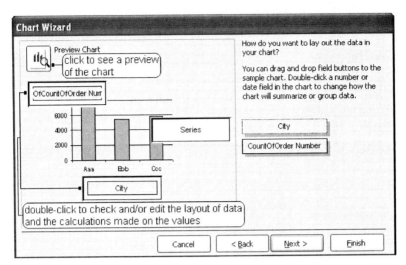

- ▷ Click **Next**.
- ▷ If necessary, delete the names that appear in the two list boxes then click the **Next** button.
- ▷ Give the chart a title, specify whether or not you want the chart to show a legend then click the **Finish** button.
- ▷ If necessary, change the size of the chart control then click 🔍 to see the chart in **Print Preview** view.
- ▷ If necessary, double-click the chart control to open the Microsoft Graph application and use the accompanying tools and commands to change the chart's presentation.
- ▷ Save the report or form then close it.

B - Inserting a bound chart into a form

A **bound chart** is a chart inserted into a form, that changes to represent each record.

Here is an example:

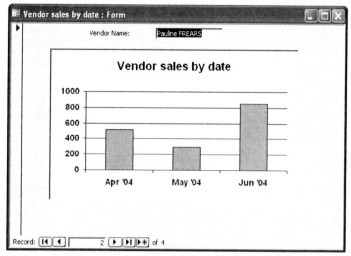

In this example, the form is linked to the Vendors table, as each record corresponds to a salesperson. The chart is based on a query which contains these fields: the vendor's name, the order date and an expression calculating the total of each order. Since the chart must be linked to each record in the form's source, a field, common to both objects, must act as a linking agent.

▷ If necessary, create the query which will form the basis of the chart. This query should contain:

- the field containing the data to be displayed on the value axis (in this case, the dates),

- the field containing the values you want to represent (in this case, the total order value),

- the field common to the source and the form, which allows a join to be established between them (in this example, the field containing the vendor number).

▷ Go into the Design view of the form concerned.

▷ **Insert - Chart**

▷ In the **Detail** section, draw a frame for the chart.

▷ Proceed as if you were creating a unbound chart (cf. previous subheading). When the wizard asks you, give the field that will link the records in the form and the chart.

▷ Finish creating the chart in the usual manner (as for an unbound chart).

C - Creating a pivot chart form

▷ To create a PivotChart AutoForm, click **Forms** in the objects bar, then click New. Click the **AutoForm: PivotChart** option, select the required table or chart from the list then click **OK**.

To create a pivot chart form in an existing form, double-click the name of the form concerned, open the list on the tool button and choose the **PivotChart View** option.

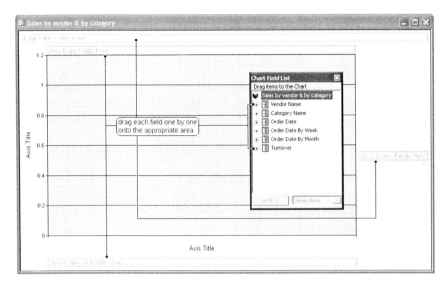

*The form chart appears in **Pivot Chart View**.*

▷ Save the form then close it.

D-Selecting an element in a pivot chart form

▷ Double-click the name of the form concerned, then if necessary, display the form in PivotChart view.

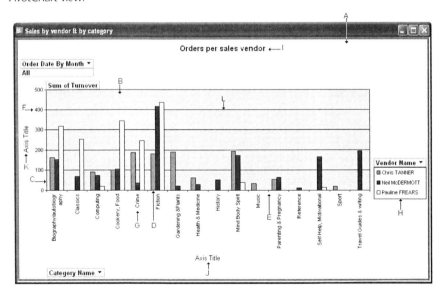

	Chart element	How to select it	What it contains
A	Chart workspace	Click the chart but not any specific item.	All the items within the chart.
B	Plot area	Click the plot area but not any specific item.	The axes and the data markers.
C	Value (Y) axis	Click one of the labels along the axis or click the axis itself.	
D	Category (X) axis	Click one of the labels along the axis or click an empty space on the axis itself.	
E	Tick marks	Cannot be selected.	Axis division markers.
F	Value axis labels	Click a label.	Y axis values, depending on the tick marks.
G	Category axis labels	Click a label.	X axis categories, depending on the tick marks.
H	Legend	To select a label in the legend, click it. To select all the labels in the legend, click any label twice.	Shows the name of the data series and contains the key for the colours used for each series' data markers.
I	Chart title	Click to select the title.	Unbound text.
J	Value axis title		
K	Category axis title		
L	Gridlines	Click one of the lines.	Lines that cross the plot area to make it easier to read chart values.

E - Changing what the pivot chart displays

▷ Double-click the name of the object concerned, then, if necessary, display the form in PivotChart view.

▷ To hide/show certain values, click the down arrow next to the field name concerned. Tick each item you want to show and deactivate all those you want to hide.

▷ To add a field, drag it from the field list window ⊞ onto the corresponding area on the pivot chart.

▷ To remove a field, point to the name of the field concerned then drag that field clear of the pivot chart. Release the mouse button when a red cross appears next to the pointer: ⬚×.

▷ Save the changes made to the object and close it.

⇨ To move a field in a pivot chart, point to the corresponding field label then drag it to the new position on the pivot chart. The mouse pointer takes a different shape depending on where in the pivot chart you drag the field label.

F- Modifying the chart type of a pivot chart

▷ Double-click the name of the object concerned, then, if necessary, display the form in PivotChart view.

▷ To modify the chart type for all the data series in the chart, click an empty space outside the plot area so that no chart item is selected. To modify the chart type for only one data series, click twice on one of the data markers in the series concerned to select all the data in that series.

▷ **PivotChart**
  Chart Type

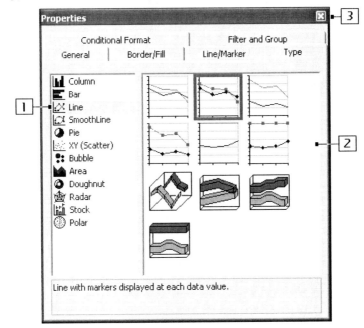

1 Select a chart type from the left hand column.

2 Click the required chart subtype.

3 Close the **Properties** dialog box.

▷ Save the changes made to the object and close it.

⇨ To transpose the series and categories (replace series by categories and vice versa), click the [⊞] tool button on the **PivotChart** toolbar.

G-Managing pivot chart titles

▷ Double-click the name of the object concerned, then, if necessary, display the form in PivotChart view.

▷ To add a title, click the element to which you wish to give a title (the chart workspace or an axis) then show its property sheet (⊞). Click the **General** tab then the ⊞ tool button in the **Add** frame. Close the **Properties** dialog box (✕).

*By default, Access adds a title, namely **Chart Workspace Title** or **Axis Title**, according to the element. You can then modify this title as you wish.*

▷ To modify a title's contents and/or position, click the title concerned to select it then show its property sheet (⊞). Click the **Format** tab and type the new title text in the **Caption** text box and/or select a new location for the title using the **Position** list. Close the **Properties** dialog box (✕).

▷ To delete a title, click the title concerned to select it then press the Del key or click ✕.

▷ Save the changes made to the object and close it.

H-Managing a pivot chart's legend

▷ Double-click the name of the object concerned, then, if necessary, display the form in PivotChart view.

▷ To show or hide the legend, activate or deactivate the ⊞ tool button or use the **PivotChart - Show Legend** command.

▷ To modify the legend's position, click the legend to select it then show its property sheet (⊞). Click the **Format** tab and select a new location for the legend using the **Position** list. Close the **Properties** dialog box (✕).

▷ Save the changes made to the object and close it.

I- Formatting a pivot chart element

▷ Double-click the name of the object concerned, then, if necessary, display the form in PivotChart view.

▷ Click the ⊞ tool button to show the **Properties** dialog box.

▷ To format a field, click the field label of the field concerned in the chart then use the tools and option under the **Format** and **Border/Fill** tabs on the property sheet.

▷ To change the font and font size of chart elements (such as category axis labels or the chart title), click the element that contains the text you want to modify then use the tools and options on the **Format** page of the property sheet.

*You will not be able to see the **Format** tab if only one category axis label is selected. You must select all the labels on the category axis by clicking a single label twice.*

▷ To change the borders and the background colours of certain chart items (such as the legend, the plot area, the chart or axis titles), click the element concerned to select it then use the tools and options on the **Border/Fill** page of the property sheet.

▷ To change the colour, line thickness or style of certain chart elements (such as the axis lines, gridlines, series lines and trendlines), click the item concerned to select it then use the tools and options on the **Line/Marker** page of the property sheet.

Access 2003

▷ To show or hide gridlines, click the axis on which you wish to display or hide the gridlines, click the **Axis** tab on the property sheet and use the options in the **Ticks and Gridlines** frame.

▷ Close the **Properties** dialog box (⊠).

▷ Save the changes made to the object and close it.

J- Managing the axes of a pivot chart

▷ Double-click the name of the object concerned, then, if necessary, display the form in PivotChart view.

▷ Click the [🖳] tool button to show the **Properties** dialog box.

▷ To add an axis, click an empty space outside the plot area so no chart element is selected then click the **Series Groups** tab. In the **Groups** list, select the group of series for which you wish to add an axis, select the **Axis position** in the appropriate list and click the **Add** button.

▷ To delete an axis, click it to select it then press the [Del] key or click [✗].

▷ To show, hide or reposition tick marks on an axis, click the axis concerned to select it then use the **Major tick marks** and **Minor tick marks** list on the **Axis** page.

▷ To change the spacing of tick marks and/or labels on the category (x) axis, click the category axis to select it then use the **Labels Spacing** and/or **Tick mark Spacing** options on the **Scale** page.

▷ To modify the intersection point between the category (x) axis and the value (y) axis, click the category axis concerned to select it then tick the **Scale** tab on the property sheet. Open the **Crosses with** list and click the option that corresponds to the axis that should intersect with the category axis. If necessary, define the intersecting point with the category axis by ticking the **Custom** check box and entering the required value in the accompanying text box.

▷ To invert the order of values on an axis, click the axis concerned to select it, then tick the **Show values in reverse order** check box on the **Scale** page.

▷ To change the scale of the value (y) axis, click the value axis concerned then the **Scale** tab. Use the **Custom max** and/or **Custom min** options to specify the highest and/or lowest value and the **Custom major unit** and **Custom minor unit** options to specify the intervals between the major and minor tick marks and the gridlines.

▷ Close the **Properties** dialog box (⊠).

▷ Save the changes made to the object and close it.

K- Showing several charts in a pivot chart form

You can create more than one pivot chart within a pivot chart form, which makes comparing your data easier.

▷ Double-click the name of the object concerned, then, if necessary, display it in Pivot Chart view.

▷ Activate the ⊞ tool button on the **PivotChart** toolbar, then, if you want to use the same scale for all the axes of the various charts, activate the ⊞ tool button.

▷ Select the field concerned in the field list then drag that field into the **Drop Multi Chart Fields Here** area. You can add several fields to a multiple chart area in this way.

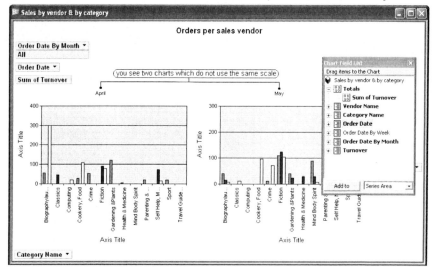

▷ Save the changes made to the object and close it.

⇒ To return to a single chart display in the pivot chart form, deactivate the ⊞ tool button on the **PivotChart** toolbar.

⇒ To define the page setup for several charts, show the property sheet ⬚, click the **General** tab then select the **Chart Workspace** option in the **Select** list. Next, choose the **Chart layout** then, if necessary, specify the **Maximum charts per row/col**.

L- Modifying the function associated with a pivot chart data field

By default, the data fields (fields that are inserted into a data area) containing numerical data use the **Sum** function and those containing other types of data, such as text, use the **Count** function.

▷ Double-click the name of the object concerned, then, if necessary, display it in Pivot Chart view.

▷ Click the name of the data field whose function you want to modify.

▷ Click the Σ tool button on the **PivotChart** toolbar and choose the required function from the list (**Sum**, **Count**, **Min**, **Max**, etc.).

▷ Save the changes made to the objet and close it.

9.1 Creating and running macros

A-Creating an independent macro

*A macro is made up of **actions**, each action corresponds to a task: when you run the macro, Access automatically carries out the actions it contains. Certain complex actions allow you to display dialog boxes, to test the answers given by the user, to display a custom menu bar, etc. By creating a macro, you create an independent application without having to do any programming (although the actions refer to instructions in the Visual Basic language).*
You can run an independent macro directly from the database window.

▷ Click **Macros** on the objects bar in the database window and click the [🗗 New] button

on the database window or open the drop-down list on the [🗗 ▼] tool button and choose **Macro** or use the **Insert - Macro** command.

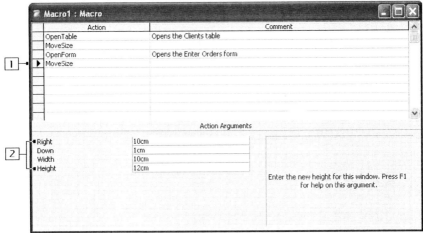

[1] Insert each action into the macro; to recognise each macro more easily, you can add a **Comment** to it.

[2] If necessary, define the arguments for each action.

▷ Save the macro as you would any other database object then close the macro window.

⇨ *A **Macro** window can contain several macros, making up a macro group.*

⇨ *To edit a macro, select its name and click the [🖉 Design] button.*

MACROS

B - Running an independent macro

▷ In any window, use the command **Tools - Macro - Run Macro**, select the **Macro Name** and click **OK**.

▷ In the macro's Design view window, click the 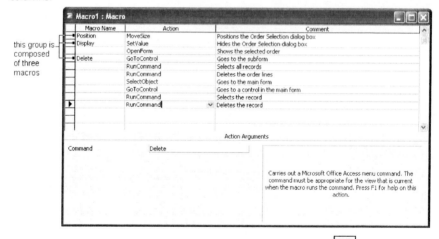 tool button.

In the database window, double-click the macro name.

*Access runs all the actions in the **Macro** window, one after another. It stops when it meets a blank line, the instruction **StopMacro** (or **StopAllMacros**), or if the macro displays a dialog box.*

⇨ *To run a macro at the opening of a database, give the macro the name **AutoExec***

(to avoid running the AutoExec macro, hold the ⌈⇧ Shift⌉ *key down while you select the database).*

⇨ *To run a macro step-by-step (to analyse how it runs), display the macro in Design*

view, click the ⌈⌐⌉ *tool button then run the macro.*

C - Creating a macro group

▷ Create a new macro, then click the ⌈⌐⌉ tool button to see the **Macro Name** column.

▷ Enter the names and the actions of all the macros in the **Macro Name** and **Action** columns.

▷ Save the macro group as you would any other database object (⌐) then close the macro window.

⇨ *To start one of the macros in the group, from any object, you have to indicate its name expressed as: **group name.macro name**. This is why the names you give to your groups and macros should be explicit, but not too long!*

D-Defining shortcut keys for running macros

▷ Create a macro group.

▷ Display the **Macro Name** column ⬚, and give the key combination you want to assign to the macro, respecting the following principles:

Symbol	Function
^	represents the Ctrl key
+	represents the ⇧ Shift key
letter or digit	represents the corresponding letter or digit key
{function}	a function key.
{key}	keys like Del or Ins

You can combine these different items: ^ A corresponds to Ctrl ***A***.

▷ In the **Action** column, enter the action(s) produced by the key combination.

▷ Save the macro group under the name **Autokeys** then close it.

▷ To run the macro, press the shortcut key combination.

E- Referring to a field/property

▷ Show the macro concerned in Design view, click the row of the action concerned, then click the text box for the required argument.

▷ To refer to a field or a control which is not in the active object, put the type of the object and its name in front of the field name, separating them with an exclamation mark (the **identifier operator**). Here are some examples:

Syntax	Function
Forms![Clients]	refers to the Clients form.
Forms![Clients]![Code]	refers to the Code field in the Clients form.
Reports![Addresses]	refers to the Addresses report.
Reports![Addresses]![LastName]	refers to the LastName field in the Addresses report.

▷ To refer to a property of a field or object, follow the field or object name by a dot and then the property name. Here are some examples:

Syntax	Function
[Code].Visible	refers to the Visible property of the Code field of the active form.
Forms![Clients].Visible	refers to the Visible property of the Clients form.
Forms![Clients]![Code].Visible	refers to the Visible property of the Code field in the Clients form.

▷ Save the changes made to the macro then close its window.

MACROS

F- Setting conditions for performing actions

▷ In the **Macro** window, click the [⊞] tool button to display the **Condition** column.

[1] Give the expression which Access will use to test the condition.

[2] Enter the actions you want performed if the condition is true. If there are several actions, type ellipses (...) in the **Condition** column, on each of the rows where an action is specified.

[3] On the next row, insert the **StopMacro** action so that the macro stops running after this first set of actions.

[4] Give the actions to be performed if the condition is false.

▷ Save the macro then close its window.

⇨ If the condition is false, Access carries out the action on the first line that does not contain ellipses.

⇨ If you leave the **StopMacro** action out, Access performs the first actions (if the condition is true) then the ones for a false condition as well!

G-Setting the value of a property with a macro

▷ Create a new macro or open an existing one in Design view.

▷ Select the **SetValue** action in the **Action** column, then give the action's arguments:

Item	If the item is a property of a control, indicate [control name].property
	If the item is a property of the active object, just give the name of the property
	If the object concerned is not active, define the item as Type object![object name].property
Expression	Give the value you want to attribute to the property.

▷ Save the changes made to the macro then close its window.

H-Getting help on integrated functions or macro actions

▷ **Help - Microsoft Office Access Help** or [F1]

▷ Open the drop-down list on the task pane title bar and choose **Search Results**, then open the drop-down list in the **Search** frame and choose the **Offline Help** option. In the search box underneath the list, type the name of the function you need help with or type the name of the macro action and click [→] to start the search.

*The various help texts appear in the **Search Results** task pane.*

Click the link of the topic you wish to see.

▷ Read the help text and, if necessary, print it.

▷ When you have finished, close the help window by clicking .

I- Setting macro security levels

Access offers you three levels of security measures, to protect you from viruses that macros can potentially contain.

▷ **Tools - Macro - Security**

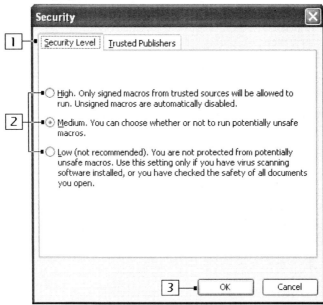

A medium security level is active by default.

| 1 | Make sure that this tab is active.

| 2 | Choose an appropriate security level by activating the correct option.

| 3 | Click to confirm.

10.1 Intranet/Internet

A-Saving an object as a Web page

▷ Open the object containing the data you want to include in a Web page, then use **File - Export**.

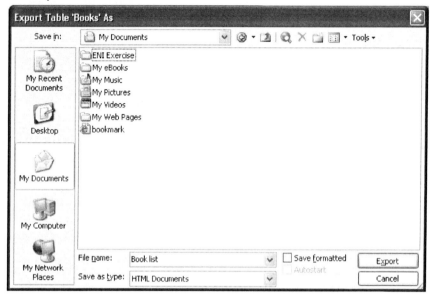

▷ Enter a name for the file in the **File name** box.

▷ Select the **HTML Documents** option as the file type.

▷ Select the folder in which you want to save the Web page and click **Export**.

B- Creating a data access page

A data access page is a Web page associated with a database.

▷ If the data access page needs to be accessible to all users on a network, place the database in a shared folder. If it is to be accessible on an intranet or the Internet, put the database into a folder beneath the root directory of the Web server.

▷ In the database window, click **Pages** in the objects bar, then click the ⊞ **New** button.

▷ Choose one of the options available, depending on how you want to create the data access page: in **Design View** or with the **Page Wizard**.

▷ In the drop-down list, select the table or query on which the data access page will be based and click **OK**.

▷ If necessary, click **OK** on the message that informs you that the data access page you are about to create cannot be opened in Design view in Access 2000.

▷ If you chose to use a wizard, follow its instructions to continue creating the data access page.
If you are working in **Design view**, a blank data access page will appear.

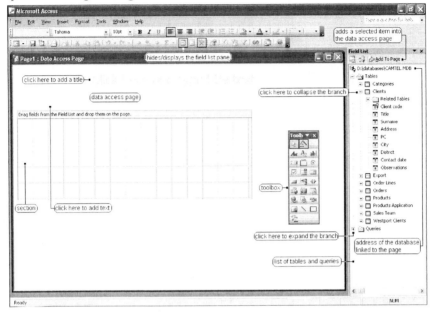

▷ Add data to the data access page by dragging each field from the **Field List** pane onto the sections of the data access page, or, if you are adding all the fields in a table or query, drag the table or query concerned.

▷ If you add an entire table or query, you should choose the appropriate option for the layout you want to give to the section into which you dragged the table/query (with the **Office Spreadsheet** option, unlike the **Columnar**, **Tabular** or **PivotTable** options, you cannot add, delete or modify data in the table). Next, click **OK**.

▷ **File - Save** or

▷ If the data access page is to be created on your hard disk, select the folder in which it must be saved. If you want it to be accessible to other users on a network, select a shared folder within that network. If you want to make it available on an intranet or the Internet, click the Web folder concerned.

▷ Specify the **File name** of the html file you want to create, then click the **Save** button.
Avoid including spaces or accents in the name of a Web or data access page.

▷ To go from Design view to Page view, use **View - Page View** or click

COMMUNICATION

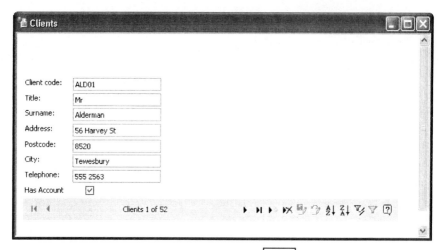

▷ To return the data access page to Design view, click [image].

▷ Save the changes made to the data access page and close it.

⇒ *The address of the database linked to the data access page is visible at the top of the* **Field List** *pane. If the database is on your hard disk, the file path takes the form* **c:\folder\database_name**. *If it is on a shared folder or Web server, the file path should take the form of a UNC path:*
\\workstation\share_name or \\Web_server\Web_folder.

⇒ *If you move the database associated with a data access page, you must change the access path to the database in the* **Select or enter a database name** *text box in the* **Data Link Properties** *dialog box (click the [image] tool button on the* **Field List** *pane then click the* **Connection** *tab).*

⇒ *It sometimes occurs that data access pages contain elements (bullets, background textures, pictures, etc.) which by default are stored in a folder called a "supporting folder" (because it contains supporting files). This folder is created in the same folder as the data access page. If you move or copy your data access page, you must also move this folder in order to preserve all links between these elements and the data access page.*

C - Grouping data in a data access page

▷ Open the data access page in Design view.

▷ If you need to, add the field where the grouping will be performed, then select its control.

▷ Click the [image] tool button.

The control moves into a new section. The ⊞ *button that appears to the left of the control indicates that grouping has been made on that control.*

▷ Click the [image] tool button to see the result in **Page** view.

118

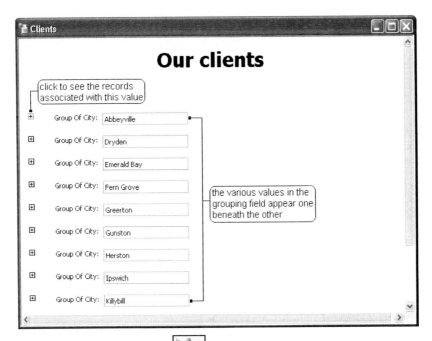

▷ To return to Design view, click the ⬜▾ tool button.

▷ Save the changes made to the data access page then close it.

D - Viewing a data access page in Internet Explorer

▷ From the source database, open the data access page in Design view then use **File - Web Page Preview**.

▷ From a workstation that has neither the source database nor Access 2003 installed, start Internet Explorer then enter the address of the data access page: if it is in a shared folder, type the address as \\workstation\shared_folder\htm_page_name .htm or if it is on a Web server, type the corresponding http address.

Access 2003 does not necessarily have to be installed but the workstation must contain Microsoft Office Web Components.

*If a dialog box appears indicating that the current security parameters prevent accessing a data source located on another domain, you need to enable the **Access data sources across domains** option in Internet Explorer (**Tools - Internet Options - Security** tab - **Custom Level** button).*

▷ Once you have consulted the page, close the browser.

E - Creating a pivot table in a data access page

A user can change the layout of a pivot table, its presentation and its calculations, but he/she cannot add, delete or modify the values it uses.

▷ Create a new data access page in Design view (without using a wizard).

COMMUNICATION

▷ Click the 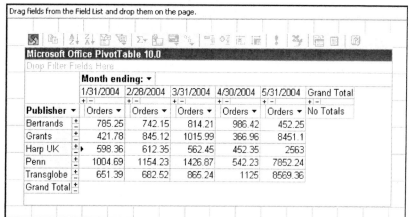 tool button in the toolbox then, on the data access page, click the spot where you want the top left corner of the control to appear.

▷ According to your requirements, define the pivot table's row, column, filter and/or detail fields. To do this, drag each individual field from the field list to the appropriate area on the pivot table.

▷ If you cannot see the entire contents of the pivot table, select the control then resize it using the selection handles (the white squares).

Drag fields from the Field List and drop them on the page.

Microsoft Office PivotTable 10.0

Drop Filter Fields Here

Month ending: ▾

Publisher ▾		1/31/2004	2/28/2004	3/31/2004	4/30/2004	5/31/2004	Grand Total
		Orders ▾	Orders ▾	Orders ▾	Orders ▾	Orders ▾	No Totals
Bertrands	±	785.25	742.15	814.21	986.42	452.25	
Grants	±	421.78	845.12	1015.99	366.96	8451.1	
Harp UK	± ▸	598.36	612.35	562.45	452.35	2563	
Penn	±	1004.69	1154.23	1426.87	542.23	7852.24	
Transglobe	±	651.39	682.52	865.24	1125	8569.36	
Grand Total	±						

▷ If necessary, specify which data you want to display or hide. To do this, click the down arrow on the field in question then tick the groups you want to display and deactivate those you want to hide then click **OK**.

▷ Save the data access page.

▷ Click the ▦ ▾ tool button to view the data access page in **Page** view.

You can also reorganise the field layout and select the data that you want to display in Page view. However, the saved presentation will still be the one that was created in Design view.

▷ To return to Design view, click the ▧ ▾ tool button.

If a filter was made in Page view, it will no longer appear in Design view.

▷ Save and close the data access page.

F - Sending a data access page as a file attachment

This technique can be used only if the database is on a server or shared workstation. The database has to be accessible to the message addressee so he/she can use the data access page correctly. The recipient does not necessarily need to have Access 2003 on his/her computer, but the Microsoft Office 2003 Web Components must be available.

▷ In the database window, click the name of the data access page that you want to send.

▷ **File - Send To - Mail Recipient (as Attachment)**

A new message window appears, to which the data access page is attached: it appears as an icon in the message window.

▷ Proceed in your usual way to prepare and send the message.

0.2 Copying/importing/exporting

A - Copying a table or query into Excel or Word and establishing a link

▷ Select the table or query concerned.

You cannot copy a selection of records.

▷ **Edit**
   Copy Ctrl C

▷ Open the Excel or Word application then the workbook or document to which you want to copy the table or query.

▷ Activate the first destination cell for the copy or put the insertion point where the copy should be placed then use **Edit - Paste Special**.

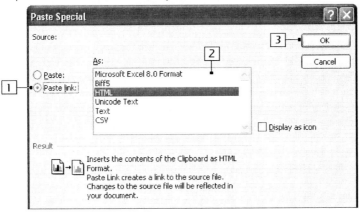

⬛1⬛ Activate this option.

⬛2⬛ Select the format in which the data must be copied.

⬛3⬛ Click to paste the copy.

▷ Save the workbook or document, if required, then close it.

⇨ *When the Excel workbook or Word document is opened, you can choose to update any changes made to the original data in Access.*

⇨ *An Access table or query can be copied into Word or Excel, without any link being made by using the traditional copying method (**Copy** and **Paste**).*

B - Exporting an object to another database

▷ Select the object concerned, then use **File - Export**.

▷ Select the destination database then click the **Export** button.

▷ Enter the name for the object you are creating in the destination database and click **OK**.

C - Exporting a report or form to Word or Excel

▷ Select the form or report concerned.

▷ Open the list on the **Office Links** tool button [image] then choose the **Publish It with Microsoft Office Word** option or the **Analyze It with Microsoft Office Excel** option.

⇨ *The Word document or Excel file is saved in the same folder as the active Access database and takes the name of the original Access report, or form, followed by an* ***.rtf*** *extension (in Word) or an* ***.xls*** *extension (in Excel).*

⇨ *If you export the form or report to Word, you can save the document in Word format (.doc) using the* ***File - Save As*** *command.*

D - Exporting data from a table or query

▷ Select the table or query that you want to export and use the **File Export** command.

▷ Open the **Save as type** list and choose the option for the application to which you want to export your table or query, such as **Microsoft Excel**, **Text Files**, **HTML Documents** or **Microsoft Office Access**.

▷ In the **File name** text box, give the name under which you want to export your data. Next, select the folder in which you want to save it (if you are creating a new file) or select the file that should receive the exported data (for an existing file). When you export to text or HTML files, you must create a new file. If you are exporting to an Access file, choose an existing file. If you are exporting to an Excel file, you can create a new workbook or choose an existing one.

▷ Click the **Export** button.

▷ If you are exporting your data in text format, the **Export Text Wizard** will open and ask you to choose an export format: **Delimited** (fields are separated by tabs, commas, semicolons or spaces) or **Fixed Width** (fields are aligned in columns and separated by spaces). Activate the required option and click **Next**.

If you choose to export in **Delimited** format, select the delimiter that will separate the fields and indicate whether or not the first row contains the field names; if you are using **Fixed Width** format, define the width of each field, following the instructions in the top frame of the dialog box.
Click **Next** then click **Finish**.

▷ If you are exporting the data to another Access database, change the name of the object that you want to create in the target database (if necessary) and click **OK**.

If you use the same name as an existing object, Access will ask you to confirm replacing that object.

E- Importing data from another application into a new table

▷ Display the database window then use **File - Get External Data - Import**.

▷ In the **Files of type** list, select the type of file containing the data you want to import: **Microsoft Excel** or **Text Files** or **HTML Documents**.

▷ Select the drive, then the folder containing the file you want to import. Click the name of the required file then click **Import** (or simply double-click the file name).

*The contents of the first wizard window vary, depending on the type of data being imported: **Text** or **Spreadsheet** or **HTML**.*

▷ If you are importing data in text format, the wizard informs you whether the text file data are **Delimited** (separated by tabs or commas) or **Fixed Width** (separated by spaces): leave the selected option active. If you are importing data from an Excel document which contains several worksheets or named ranges, activate the **Show Worksheets** option and select the worksheet containing the required data or activate the **Show Named Ranges** option and select the name of the range containing the data you want.

▷ Click the **Next** button to go to the next step.

▷ If you are importing text file data in a **Delimited** format, select the delimiter that will separate the fields then specify if the **First Row Contains Field Names**. If the data are of **Fixed Width**, define the width of the field following the instructions contained in the window's first frame. If the imported data come from an Excel file, specify if the **First Row Contains Column Headings** then, if required, click **OK** on the message that offers to change field names that are not valid as Access field names.

▷ Click the **Next** button to go to the next step.

▷ If you want to import the data into a new table, activate the **In a New Table** option. To place them in an existing table, activate the **In an Existing Table** option and choose that table's name from the drop-down list.

▷ Click **Next** to go on to the next step.

▷ If you are importing into a new table, set the options for each field you are importing; if any field should not be imported into the new table, activate the **Do not import field (Skip)** option and click **Next**.

▷ If you need to define a primary key for the new table, activate the first option, if you want Access to add one for you, or the second option if you wish to choose a primary key from the drop-down list. If you do not want to set any primary key, activate the **No primary key** option.

▷ If you chose to import the data into a new table, enter the table name in the **Import to Table** text box and click **Finish**.

▷ If you are importing into an existing table, do not change the contents of the **Import to Table** text box but click the **Finish** button straight away.

▷ Click **OK**.

F- Managing data from another Access database

Access offers two techniques for managing data from another database: importing an object or linking a table. Linking a table has the advantage of enabling you to work in the table in its source application. You can also create, in Access, queries, forms or reports based on linked tables. This approach enables you to work with the data on a real time basis (or even modify data in a linked table).

▷ Display the database window then use **File - Get External Data - Import** or **Link Tables**.

▷ Select the database file concerned then click the **Import** or **Link** button.

▷ Select the name of the object you wish to import or the name of the table you are linking.

▷ If you are importing an object, you may like to click the **Options** button to change the import options.

▷ Click **OK**.

⇨ *If you import a table, Access creates a new table of the same name as the file. If you link a table, a special symbol appears in Access to indicate that this is a linked table. Furthermore, any changes made in the table are carried over into the Excel list or in the text file and vice versa.*

A

B

C

D

E

INDEX